The Complete Indonesian Cookbook

Authentic Indonesian Recipes Make Traditional Indonesian Cooking Easy, Quick and Tasty

BY: LAURA G. MYLES

TABLE OF CONTENTS

RECIPES

1.Nasi Uduk (Coconut Rice):

Prep Time: 15 mins

Cook Time: 25 mins

Total Time: 40 mins

Servings: 4

Ingredients:

- 2 cups of jasmine rice
- 1 3/4 cups of coconut milk
- 1 stalk lemongrass, bruised
- 2 kaffir lime leaves
- 1 tsp salt
- 1/2 tsp turmeric powder

Instructions:

1. Drain the rice after a thorough wash.
2. Rice, coconut milk, lemongrass, kaffir lime leaves, salt, and turmeric powder Must all be combined in a rice cooker.
3. As directed by your rice cooker, prepare the rice.
4. When the rice is finished cooking, separate the grains by fluffing it with a fork.
5. Before serving, take the lemongrass and kaffir lime leaves out.

Nutrition (per serving):

Cals: 320, Carbs: 44g

Protein: 4g, Fat: 15g, Fiber: 1g

2. Ayam Betutu (Balinese Spiced Chicken):

Prep Time: 30 mins

Cook Time: 2 hrs

Total Time: 2 hrs 30 mins

Servings: 4

Ingredients:

- 1 whole chicken (about 3-4 lbs)
- 10 shallots
- 5 cloves garlic
- 5 red chillies
- 2 tsp shrimp paste
- 1 tsp turmeric powder
- 1 tsp ginger
- 1 tsp galangal
- 2 lemongrass stalks, bruised
- Banana leaves for wrapping

Instructions:

1. To produce a spice paste, combine shallots, garlic, red chilies, shrimp paste, turmeric powder, ginger, and galangal.
2. Cleanse the chicken thoroughly, then massage it all over with the spice paste. Give it an hr to marinate.
3. With kitchen twine, enclose the chicken in banana leaves.
4. The chicken Must be steamed or baked for about two hrs, or up to cooked, at 350°F (175°C).
5. The chicken Must be unwrapped after cooking and quickly grilled for a smokey taste before dishing.

Nutrition (per serving):

Cals: 380, Carbs: 10g, Protein: 30g

Fat: 25g, Fiber: 2g

3. Tempeh Goreng (Fried Tempeh):

Prep Time: 15 mins

Cook Time: 15 mins

Total Time: 30 mins

Servings: 4

Ingredients:

- 8 oz tempeh, slice into thin slices
- Oil for frying
- Salt as needed

Instructions:

1. Oil in a pan is heated to medium heat.
2. The tempeh slices Must be crisp and golden brown after frying.
3. Take out and drain on paper towels after leaving the oil.
4. While the food is still hot, salt it.
5. Serve on its own or in various meals.

Nutrition (per serving):

Cals: 180, Carbs: 9g, Protein: 15g

Fat: 10g, Fiber: 5g

4. Pepes Ikan (Steamed Fish in Banana Leaves):

Prep Time: 20 mins

Cook Time: 30 mins

Total Time: 50 mins

Servings: 4

Ingredients:

- 1 lb fish fillets (snapper, grouper, or mackerel), slice into pieces
- Banana leaves, slice into squares and blanched
- 2 tomatoes, thinly split
- 1 lemongrass stalk, bruised and chop-up
- 4 kaffir lime leaves, thinly split
- 4 shallots, thinly split
- 3 cloves garlic, chop-up

- 1 tsp turmeric powder
- Salt as needed

Instructions:

1. Combine salt and turmeric powder with the fish.
2. Put some fish in the middle of a piece of banana leaf and place it somewhere flat.
3. Slices of tomato, lemongrass, kaffir lime leaves, shallots, and garlic are placed on top.
4. With toothpicks or twine, create a pouch out of the banana leaf and the ingredients.
5. To cook and flavor the fish, steam the packets for 20 to 30 mins.

Nutrition (per serving):

Cals: 220, Carbs: 10g, Protein: 20g

Fat: 10g, Fiber: 2g

5. Sambal Matah (Balinese Raw Sambal):

Prep Time: 15 mins

Cook Time: 0 mins

Total Time: 15 mins

Servings: 4

Ingredients:

- 5 shallots, thinly split
- 5 red chillies, thinly split
- 2-3 bird's eye chillies, thinly split (adjust to your spice preference)
- 2 lemongrass stalks, thinly split (only the tender parts)
- 3 kaffir lime leaves, thinly split
- 1 tsp shrimp paste, toasted
- 1 tsp salt
- 1 tsp sugar
- 2 tbsp lime juice

Instructions:

1. In a bowl, combine all the split ingredients.
2. Salt and shrimp paste Must be blended into a smooth paste in a mortar and pestle.
3. To the bowl of split items, add the shrimp paste combination, sugar, and lime juice.
4. Combine everything by tossing it together thoroughly.
5. Prior to serving, give the flavors 10 mins to blend.

Nutrition (per serving):

Cals: 25, Carbs: 6g, Protein: 1g

Fat: 0g, Fiber: 1g

6.Nasi Goreng (Indonesian Fried Rice)

Prep Time: 15 mins

Cook Time: 15 mins

Total Time: 30 mins

Servings: 4

Ingredients:

- 3 cups of cooked rice, preferably cold and day-old
- 200g chicken breast, diced
- 2 eggs, beaten
- 1 cup of combined vegetables (carrots, peas, corn)
- 3 cloves garlic, chop-up
- 2 shallots, lightly chop-up
- 2 tbsp vegetable oil
- 2 tbsp sweet soy sauce (kecap manis)
- 1 tbsp soy sauce
- 1 tsp shrimp paste (non-compulsory)
- Salt and pepper as needed
- Split cucumber and tomato for garnish
- Fried shallots for garnish

Instructions:

1. In a wok or sizable skillet, heat the vegetable oil over medium-high heat. Add the chop-up shallots and chop-up garlic, and cook up to fragrant.
2. Cook the chicken up to it's no longer pink and fully cooked after adding the diced chicken. To one side of the wok, push the chicken.
3. In the empty side of the wok, add the beaten eggs and scramble them up to they are done.
4. The combined veggies Must be stir-fried for a few mins up to they are just beginning to soften.
5. Break up any clumps before adding the cooled rice to the wok. Combine all the ingredients.
6. Rice Must be covered with shrimp paste (if using), regular soy sauce, and sweet soy sauce. Stir-fry the sauces to blend and distribute them equally.
7. As needed, add salt and pepper to the food. Stir-frying Must continue for a few more mins or up to everything is thoroughly combined and cooked.
8. Place the Nasi Goreng on plates and top with fried shallots, tomato slices, and cucumber slices as garnish.

NUTRITION INFO: (per serving)

Cals: 425 kcal, Carbs: 62g, Protein: 18g

Fat: 11g, Fiber: 3g

7. Rendang (Sumatran Beef Stew)

Prep Time: 20 mins

Cook Time: 3 hrs

Total Time: 3 hrs 20 mins

Servings: 6

Ingredients:

- 1 kg beef, slice into chunks
- 2 cans (400ml every) coconut milk
- 2 lemongrass stalks, bruised
- 4 kaffir lime leaves
- 2 turmeric leaves (if available), torn (non-compulsory)
- 1 cinnamon stick
- 3 cardamom pods
- 3 cloves
- 2 star anise
- 2 tbsp tamarind paste
- 1 tbsp brown sugar
- Salt as needed
- 3 tbsp vegetable oil

Instructions:

1. Over medium heat, warm the vegetable oil in a big pot. Brown the meat chunks all over after adding them. Take out and place aside.
2. The spices (cinnamon, cardamom, cloves, and star anise) Must be added to the same saucepan and sautéed up to fragrant.
3. Browned beef Must be added back to the pot. Add the tamarind paste, brown sugar, salt, lemongrass, kaffir lime leaves, turmeric leaves (if using), and coconut milk.
4. Heat Must be turned down once the Mixture comes to a boil. For around three hrs, with the lid on, the stew Must simmer up to the beef is soft and the sauce has thickened. sometimes stir.
5. Cook the beef uncovered while sometimes stirring up to the sauce is thick and coats the meat after the meat is cooked and the sauce has reduced.
6. Serve steamed rice alongside the rendang.

NUTRITION INFO: (per serving)

Cals: 490 kcal, Carbs: 7g, Protein: 32g

Fat: 38g, Fiber: 1g

8.Babi Guling (Balinese Suckling Pig)

Prep Time: 1 hr

Cook Time: 4 hrs

Total Time: 5 hrs

Servings: 6-8

Ingredients:

- 1 whole suckling pig (about 20-25 lbs)
- 10 cloves garlic, chop-up
- 2 tbsp turmeric powder
- 1 tbsp coriander powder
- 1 tbsp white pepper
- 1 tbsp salt
- 5 stalks lemongrass, bruised
- 5 kaffir lime leaves
- Banana leaves for wrapping
- Cooking twine

Instructions:

1. Take out any extra fat and organs before cleaning and preparing the suckling pig.
2. To make a paste, combine the chop-up garlic, salt, white pepper, turmeric, and coriander powder in a bowl.
3. Inside and out, rub the pig with the spice paste.
4. Fill the pig's cavity with kaffir lime and lemongrass leaves.
5. The pig Must be wrapped in banana leaves and tied with cooking twine.
6. The pig Must be roasted for about 4 hrs at 325°F (165°C), or up to the skin is crispy and the meat is soft.
7. Just a few mins Must pass before Cutting and serving the pig.

Nutrition (per serving):

Cals: ~600, Protein: ~30g, Fat: ~45g, Carbs: ~10g

9. Soto Betawi (Jakarta Beef Soup)

Prep Time: 20 mins

Cook Time: 2 hrs

Total Time: 2 hrs 20 mins

Servings: 4-6

Ingredients:

- 1 lb beef, slice into bite-sized pieces
- 2 lemongrass stalks, bruised
- 4 kaffir lime leaves
- 2 bay leaves
- 1-inch galangal, split
- 3 cloves garlic, chop-up
- 1 onion, chop-up
- 1 tsp coriander powder
- 1/2 tsp turmeric powder
- 1/2 tsp white pepper
- 4 cups of beef broth
- 1 cup of coconut milk
- Salt as needed
- Cooking oil
- Rice vermicelli, cooked according to box/pkg instructions
- Bean sprouts, lime wedges, and fried shallots for garnish

Instructions:

1. Cooking oil Must be heated in a pot before sautéing garlic and onion up to aromatic.
2. Once beef has been added, brown it. White pepper, turmeric, and coriander powder Must be added. Combine thoroughly.
3. Add galangal, bay leaves, lemongrass, and kaffir lime leaves. Coconut milk and beef broth Must be added.
4. For about two hrs, simmer the soup over low heat to let the flavors meld and the beef become soft. As needed, add salt.
5. Over cooked rice vermicelli, top the soup with bean sprouts, lime wedges, and fried shallots for decoration.

Nutrition (per serving):

Cals: ~350, Protein: ~20g, Fat: ~20g, Carbs: ~25g

10. Sate Ayam (Chicken Satay)

Prep Time: 20 mins

Cook Time: 10 mins

Total Time: 30 mins

Servings: 4

Ingredients:

- 1 lb (450g) boneless chicken breasts, slice into thin strips
- 2 tbsp soy sauce
- 2 tbsp kecap manis (sweet soy sauce)
- 1 tbsp vegetable oil
- 1 tsp ground coriander
- 1 tsp ground cumin
- 1 tsp turmeric
- 2 cloves garlic, chop-up
- Wooden skewers, soaked in water

Instructions:

1. To make the marinade, combine the soy sauce, kecap manis, vegetable oil, turmeric, ground cumin, and chop-up garlic in a bowl.
2. The moistened wooden skewers are then threaded with the chicken strips.
3. Pour the marinade over the chicken skewers after placing them in a shlet dish. Give the chicken a thorough coating and marinate it for at least an hr.
4. The grill or grill pan Must be preheated to medium-high heat.
5. The chicken skewers Must be cooked through and slightly browned after grilling them for 3 to 5 mins on every side.
6. Serve rice and the chicken satay with the peanut sauce.

Nutrition (per serving):

Cals: 250, Protein: 28g

Carbs: 10g

Fat: 10g, Fiber: 1g

11. Gado-Gado (Indonesian Salad with Peanut Sauce)

Prep Time: 20 mins

Cook Time: 10 mins

Total Time: 30 mins

Servings: 4

Ingredients:

- 4 cups of combined vegetables (bean sprouts, cabbage, spinach, long beans, carrots), blanched
- 1 cup of tofu, cubed and fried
- 1 cup of tempeh, split and fried
- 2 hard-boiled eggs, halved
- 1 cup of cooked rice or rice cakes
- 1/2 cup of fried shallots
- 1/2 cup of prawn crackers (non-compulsory)
- Peanut Sauce:
- 1 cup of peanuts, roasted and ground
- 2 cloves garlic, chop-up
- 1 tsp tamarind paste
- 1 tbsp palm sugar or brown sugar
- 1/2 cup of water
- 1 tbsp soy sauce
- 1/2 tsp chili powder (adjust as needed)

Instructions:

1. To make the peanut sauce, combine palm sugar, water, soy sauce, chili powder, tamarind paste, chop-up garlic, and ground peanuts in a pot. Cook the sauce up to it thickens over low heat. When necessary, add extra water.
2. Place the fried tofu, fried tempeh, hard-boiled eggs, cooked rice, and rice cakes on serving dishes along with the blanched veggies.
3. Sprinkle the vegetables and other toppings with the peanut sauce.
4. If used, garnish with fried shallots and prawn crackers.
5. Gado-Gado Must be served quickly.

Nutrition (per serving, including peanut sauce):

Cals: 450, Protein: 20g

Carbs: 40g, Fat: 26g, Fiber: 8g

12. Sambal Oelek (Chili Paste)

Prep Time: 15 mins

Cook Time: 15 mins

Total Time: 30 mins

Servings: Makes about 1 cup of

Ingredients:

- 10-15 red chili peppers, stemmed and roughly chop-up
- 3 cloves garlic, peel off
- 1 tsp salt
- 1 tsp sugar
- 1 tbsp lime juice

Instructions:

1. Combine the chili peppers, garlic, salt, and sugar in a mixer up to a rough paste forms.
2. In a mini saucepan, add the paste, and simmer, stirring regularly, for 10 to 15 mins at medium heat.
3. Take it off the stove and let it cool.
4. Add lime juice and taste-test before adding salt and sugar.
5. Place in the refrigerator in a sterile jar.

Nutrition (per tbsp):

Cals: 10, Carbs: 2g, Fiber: 0.5g, Protein: 0.3g

Fat: 0.1g, Sodium: 186mg

13.Ketoprak (Jakarta Rice Noodle Salad)

Prep Time: 20 mins

Cook Time: 10 mins

Total Time: 30 mins

Servings: 4

Ingredients:

- 200g rice noodles, cooked and drained
- 100g bean sprouts
- 100g firm tofu, fried and cubed
- 2 boiled eggs, split
- 2 tbsp sweet soy sauce (kecap manis)
- 2 tbsp peanut oil
- 1/4 cup of peanuts, roasted and chop-up
- 2 cloves garlic, chop-up
- Salt and pepper as needed

Instructions:

1. Rice noodles, bean sprouts, tofu, and boiled eggs Must all be combined in a big bowl.
2. Combine sweet soy sauce, peanut oil, chop-up garlic, salt, and pepper in a mini bowl.
3. Toss the noodles with the sauce after pouring it over them.
4. Add chop-up peanuts on top.
5. Serve right away.

Nutrition (per serving):

Cals: 320, Carbs: 32g

Fiber: 2.5g, Protein: 13g, Fat: 17g, Sodium: 410mg

14. Sate Padang (Padang-style Satay)

Prep Time: 20 mins

Cook Time: 30 mins

Total Time: 50 mins

Servings: 4

Ingredients:

- 500g beef, thinly split into mini pieces
- 2 lemongrass stalks, white parts only, bruised
- 4 kaffir lime leaves
- 1 tbsp tamarind paste
- 1 tbsp sweet soy sauce (kecap manis)
- 1 tsp ground turmeric
- Salt and pepper as needed

Instructions:

1. To make a marinade, combine the tamarind paste, sweet soy sauce, ground turmeric, salt, and pepper in a basin.
2. Slices of beef Must be added to the marinade, thoroughly coated, and left to marinate for 15 to 20 mins.
3. Lemongrass and kaffir lime leaf pieces are alternated with threadings of the marinated beef onto the skewers.
4. The skewers Must be cooked through and slightly browned after grilling or broiling for 8 to 10 mins, turning them once.
5. Give extra sweet soy sauce for dipping and serve with rice.

Nutrition (per serving):

Cals: 240, Carbs: 5g

Fiber: 1g, Protein: 30g, Fat: 10g, Sodium: 490mg

15. Rujak Buah (Indonesian Fruit Salad)

Prep Time: 15 mins

Total Time: 15 mins

Servings: 4

Ingredients:

- 2 cups of combined tropical fruits (pineapple, mango, papaya, etc), peel off and diced
- 1 cucumber, peel off and split
- 1/2 cup of roasted peanuts, coarsely chop-up
- 1 mini red chili pepper, split (non-compulsory for heat)
- 2 tbsp tamarind pulp, soaked in 1/4 cup of warm water
- 2 tbsp palm sugar or brown sugar
- Salt as needed

Instructions:

1. Combine the tamarind pulp and warm water in a mini bowl. To obtain the tamarind juice, strain.
2. Combine the diced fruits, cucumber slices, and chili pepper slices in a sizable bowl.
3. The palm sugar, tamarind juice, and a dash of salt Must all be combined in another mini basin. To make the dressing, thoroughly combine.
4. The fruit combination will be covered with the dressing; gently toss to blend.
5. The salad Must be topped with chop-up peanuts.
6. As an energizing side dish or snack, serve right away.

Nutrition (per serving):

Cals: 160, Carbs: 27g, Fiber: 3g, Protein: 4g

Fat: 5g, Sodium: 80mg

16. Soto Ayam (Chicken Soup)

Prep Time: 20 mins

Cook Time: 1 hr

Total Time: 1 hr 20 mins

Servings: 4

Ingredients:

- 500g bone-in chicken pieces
- 4 cups of chicken broth
- 2 lemongrass stalks, bruised
- 3 kaffir lime leaves
- 1 inch ginger, split
- 2 cloves garlic, chop-up
- 1 tsp turmeric powder
- Salt and pepper as needed
- Rice vermicelli, cooked
- Bean sprouts
- Boiled eggs, halved
- Fried shallots
- Lime wedges

Instructions:

1. Chicken, chicken broth, ginger, garlic, turmeric powder, salt, and pepper are all combined in a saucepan with lemongrass, kaffir lime leaves, and chicken.
2. Up to the chicken is cooked and tender, bring to a boil, then lower the heat and simmer for a while.
3. Chicken Must be taken out of the soup, the meat shredded, and left aside.
4. Return the broth to the pot after straining the solids out.
5. When ready to serve, put cooked rice vermicelli and shredded chicken in bowls and top with hot broth.
6. Bean sprouts, cooked egg halves, fried shallots, and lime wedges Must be added on top.

Nutrition (per serving):

Cals: ~300, Protein: ~20g, Carbs: ~25g, Fat: ~12g

17. Pempek Palembang (Fishcake in Spicy Sauce)

Prep Time: 30 mins

Cook Time: 30 mins

Total Time: 1 hr

Servings: 6

Ingredients:

- 500g fish fillets, ground
- 150g sago flour
- 2 cloves garlic, chop-up
- Salt and pepper as needed
- Cooking oil for frying
- Spicy Sauce:
- 3 tbsp vinegar
- 3 tbsp soy sauce
- 2 tbsp chili sauce
- 1 tbsp sugar
- 1 clove garlic, chop-up

Instructions:

1. Garlic powder, sago flour, ground fish, salt, and pepper Must all be thoroughly blended in a basin.
2. Create mini oval or round patties out of the ingredients.
3. The fishcakes Must be cooked completely and golden brown after being fried in hot oil.
4. Vinegar, soy sauce, chili sauce, sugar, and chop-up garlic are combined to make the sauce in a bowl.
5. Serve the spicy sauce beside the fried fishcakes.

Nutrition (per serving):

Cals: ~250, Protein: ~15g, Carbs: ~25g

Fat: ~10g

18. Bakmi Goreng (Fried Noodles)

Prep Time: 15 mins

Cook Time: 15 mins

Total Time: 30 mins

Servings: 4

Ingredients:

- 250g egg noodles
- 150g chicken breast, split
- 100g shrimp, peel off and deveined
- 2 cloves garlic, chop-up
- 1 mini onion, split
- 1 carrot, julienned
- 1/2 cup of cabbage, shredded
- 2 tbsp soy sauce

- 1 tbsp oyster sauce
- 1 tsp sesame oil
- 2 eggs, beaten
- Salt and pepper as needed
- Oil for cooking

Instructions:

1. The egg noodles Must be prepared as directed on the packaging. Drain, then set apart.
2. Heat some oil over medium-high heat in a big pan or wok. Add the onion slices and garlic powder. up to fragrant, sauté.
3. Shrimp and chicken slices Must be added to the pan. Cook the shrimp up to they become pink and curl, and the chicken is no longer pink.
4. To the side of the pan, push the cooked chicken and shrimp. After adding the beaten eggs, scramble them up to they are done.
5. To the pan, add the shredded cabbage and julienned carrots. Stir-fry the vegetables for a few mins, or up to they begin to soften.
6. Add the cooked egg noodles together with the sesame oil, soy sauce, and oyster sauce. All the ingredients Must be thoroughly combined to distribute the sauces throughout the noodles.
7. As needed, add salt and pepper to the food. Stir-fry for a further two to three mins.
8. Serve the Bakmi Goreng hot with extras like fried shallots and thinly split green onions.

NUTRITION INFO:

Cals: ~400 per serving, Protein: ~20g

Carbs: ~40g, Fat: ~15g

19. Sop Buntut (Oxtail Soup)

Prep Time: 20 mins

Cook Time: 3 hrs

Total Time: 3 hrs 20 mins

Servings: 6

Ingredients:

- 1 kg oxtail, slice into pieces
- 1 onion, chop-up
- 3 cloves garlic, chop-up
- 2 carrots, peel off and split
- 2 potatoes, peel off and diced
- 2 tomatoes, chop-up
- 2 stalks celery, chop-up
- 2 bay leaves
- 1 lemongrass stalk, bruised
- 1 tsp black peppercorns
- Salt as needed
- 2 tbsp oil
- Water
- Fried shallots and chop-up cilantro for garnish

Instructions:

1. Over medium heat, warm the oil in a big pot. Sauté the chop-up garlic and onion up to aromatic.
2. Add the oxtail chunks and sauté them up to all sides are browned.
3. Fill the pot with water so that the oxtail is submerged. Black peppercorns, lemongrass, and bay leaves Must be added. Bring to a boil, then lower the heat to a simmer, cover the pot, and cook the oxtail for about two hrs, or up to it is soft.
4. To the pot, add the diced potatoes, diced tomatoes, chop-up celery, and carrots. Once the vegetables are tender, simmer for a further 30 to 40 mins.
5. As needed, add salt to the soup. Eliminate the lemongrass stem and bay leaves.
6. Serve the Sop Buntut hot with chop-up cilantro and fried shallots as garnish.

NUTRITION INFO:

Cals: ~400 per serving, Protein: ~30g

Carbs: ~20g, Fat: ~25g

20. Tahu Telur (Tofu Omelette)

Prep Time: 15 mins

Cook Time: 15 mins

Total Time: 30 mins

Servings: 4

Ingredients:

- 200g firm tofu, cubed
- 4 eggs
- 1 mini onion, thinly split
- 2 cloves garlic, chop-up
- 2 green onions, chop-up
- 2 tbsp cooking oil
- Salt and pepper as needed

Instructions:

1. Whisk the eggs in a bowl up to completely combined. Add a little salt and pepper for seasoning.
2. In a pan, heat 1 tbsp of oil over medium heat. Cubed tofu Must be added and cooked up to golden brown all around. Take out and place aside.
3. Add the last tbsp of oil to the same pan. Garlic and onion slices are sautéed up to aromatic.
4. Return the cooked tofu to the pan and top with the whisked eggs.
5. The eggs Must be cooked and slightly set before being gently scrambled and combined with the tofu.

6. Cook the eggs more up to they are fully cooked and set.
7. Add chop-up green onions as a garnish.
8. Steamed rice and a dish of Sambal Kecap Must be served with the Tahu Telur.

Nutrition (per serving):
Cals: ~250 kcal, Protein: ~15g
Carbs: ~10g, Fat: ~17g

21. Sayur Lodeh (Coconut Vegetable Stew)

Prep Time: 20 mins
Cook Time: 30 mins
Total Time: 50 mins
Servings: 6

Ingredients:
- 1 cup of coconut milk
- 2 cups of combined vegetables (e.g., long beans, cabbage, carrot), slice into bite-sized pieces
- 200g tofu, cubed
- 1 mini eggplant, split
- 2 cloves garlic, chop-up
- 1 mini onion, chop-up
- 2 tbsp vegetable oil
- 1 tsp turmeric powder
- 1 tsp ground coriander
- Salt and sugar as needed

Instructions:
1. Over medium heat, warm the vegetable oil in a saucepan. Sauté the chop-up garlic and onion up to aromatic.
2. Add the ground coriander and turmeric powder. To blend, thoroughly stir.
3. Add the coconut milk, then gently boil the Mixture.
4. Add the tofu, eggplant, and combined vegetables. Cook the vegetables up to they are soft.
5. To balance the flavors, sprinkle on some salt and a dash of sugar.
6. Take out the pot from the heat once the vegetables are done cooking.
7. Steamed rice Must be served with the Sayur Lodeh.

Nutrition (per serving):
Cals: ~200 kcal, Protein: ~5g
Carbs: ~15g, Fat: ~15g

22. Bubur Sumsum (Rice Porridge with Palm Sugar)

Prep Time: 5 mins
Cook Time: 30 mins
Total Time: 35 mins
Servings: 4

Ingredients:
- 1 cup of rice flour
- 4 cups of water
- 1/2 cup of palm sugar, shaved or chop-up
- 1/4 cup of coconut milk
- A pinch of salt
- Finely grated coconut for topping

Instructions:
1. Rice flour and a little water Must be combined in a bowl to create a smooth paste.
2. Bring the remaining water to a boil in a kettle. Add the rice flour paste gradually, stirring constantly to avoid lumps.
3. Till the Mixture thickens into a smooth porridge, simmer the Mixture over a low heat while stirring often.
4. When the palm sugar has been added and thoroughly combined in, the porridge is sweet.
5. Add a dash of salt and the coconut milk after stirring. Combine thoroughly.
6. Take the pot off the stove.
7. Warm Bubur Sumsum Must be served with finely grated coconut on top.

Nutrition (per serving):
Cals: ~250 kcal, Protein: ~2g
Carbs: ~60g, Fat: ~1g

23. Sambal Kecap (Sweet Soy Sauce with Chilies)

Prep Time: 10 mins
Cook Time: 5 mins
Total Time: 15 mins
Servings: Makes about 1/2 cup of

Ingredients:
- 1/2 cup of sweet soy sauce (kecap manis)
- 3 red chilies, thinly split
- 2 cloves garlic, chop-up
- 1 tbsp lime juice

Instructions:
1. Heat a tiny quantity of oil in a mini pan over medium heat.
2. Red chiles, slice into slices, and chop-up garlic are added. Sauté for a few mins, or up to fragrant and just beginning to soften.
3. To the pan, add the sweet soy sauce (kecap manis). To blend, thoroughly stir.

4. Leting the flavors to mingle, boil the Mixture for around two to three mins.
5. Once the sambal kecap has slightly cooled, take out the pan from the fire.
6. To give it a tart kick, stir in the lime juice.
7. To serve, place the sambal kecap in a mini dish.

Nutrition (per serving - 1 tbsp):
Cals: ~30 kcal, Protein: ~1g
Carbs: ~6g, Fat: ~0g

24.Pecel Lele (Fried Catfish with Peanut Sauce)

Prep Time: 20 mins
Cook Time: 20 mins
Total Time: 40 mins
Servings: 4

Ingredients:
- 4 catfish fillets
- 1 cup of rice flour
- Salt and pepper as needed
- Oil for frying
- For the peanut sauce:
- 1 cup of roasted peanuts, lightly ground
- 2 cloves garlic, chop-up
- 2 red chili peppers, chop-up
- 1 tbsp tamarind paste
- 2 tbsp sweet soy sauce
- Salt and sugar as needed
- For serving:
- Cooked rice
- Split cucumber and tomato

Instructions:
1. The catfish fillets Must be washed and pat dried. Add salt and pepper as needed.
2. Shake off any excess rice flour before coating the catfish fillets.
3. In a frying pan, heat the oil over medium-low heat. The catfish fillets Must be fried up to crispy and golden. Take out, then dry off with paper towels.
4. To make the peanut sauce, combine the sweet soy sauce, salt, sugar, tamarind paste, chop-up garlic, chop-up jalapeño peppers, and ground peanuts in a bowl. To revery the correct consistency, gradually add water.
5. Along with cooked rice, cucumber and tomato slices, peanut sauce, and the fried catfish, serve.

Nutrition (per serving):
Cals: ~380, Protein: ~20g, Fat: ~15g
Carbs: ~40g, Fiber: ~3g

25. Asam Pedas (Spicy Sour Fish Stew)

Prep Time: 15 mins
Cook Time: 25 mins
Total Time: 40 mins
Servings: 4

Ingredients:
- 500g fish fillets (snapper, mackerel, or any firm fish), slice into chunks
- 2 tomatoes, split
- 2 stalks lemongrass, bruised
- 4 kaffir lime leaves
- 3 tbsp tamarind paste
- 2 tbsp oil
- 1 tsp shrimp paste (non-compulsory)
- 2 tsp sugar
- Salt as needed
- For the spice paste:
- 5 shallots
- 3 cloves garlic
- 5 red chili peppers
- 2 red bird's eye chili peppers (adjust as needed)
- 1 inch galangal or ginger
- 1 tsp turmeric powder

Instructions:
1. The spice paste ingredients Must be processed in a mixer up to smooth.
2. Oil in a pot is heated to medium heat. The shrimp paste and spice paste Must be cooked up to aromatic.
3. Fish chunks Must be added and cooked up to they begin to turn opaque.
4. Including tomatoes, tamarind paste, kaffir lime leaves, sugar, and salt. Stir thoroughly.
5. Add enough water to the ingredients to cover them. Simmer for a while to let the flavors combine and the fish cook.
6. If necessary, adjust the seasoning. Get rid of the heat.
7. Along with steaming rice, serve the asam pedas.

Nutrition (per serving):
Cals: ~220, Protein: ~20g
Fat: ~8g, Carbs: ~18g, Fiber: ~3g

26. Es Cendol (Coconut Milk Drink)

Prep Time: 10 mins
Cook Time: 10 mins
Total Time: 20 mins
Servings: 4

Ingredients:
- 1 cup of rice flour

- 1/4 cup of pandan juice (screwpine leaves extract)
- 1/2 cup of coconut milk
- 1/2 cup of palm sugar, dilute in 1/4 cup of water
- Ice cubes
- Water

Instructions:

1. Combine pandan juice with rice flour. Stir thoroughly to combine.
2. Big pot of water is boiling. To create the cendol strands, push the rice flour Mixture through a strainer with lots of holes and into the boiling water. The cendol strands need to cook for a few mins. Rinse with cold water after draining.
3. Put a few ice cubes and a tsp of cendol strands in serving glasses.
4. Combine the palm sugar syrup with the coconut milk. Over the cendol and ice, pour the concoction.
5. Just before enjoying, gently stir.

Nutrition (per serving):
Cals: ~220, Protein: ~1g, Fat: ~6g
Carbs: ~40g, Fiber: ~0g

27. Perkedel Kentang (Potato Fritters)

Prep Time: 20 mins

Cook Time: 20 mins

Total Time: 40 mins

Servings: 4

Ingredients:

- 4 Big potatoes, boiled and mashed
- 1 egg
- 3 tbsp all-purpose flour
- 2 cloves garlic, chop-up
- 2 green onions, lightly chop-up
- Salt and pepper as needed
- Oil for frying

Instructions:

1. Mash potatoes with egg, all-purpose flour, chop-up garlic, green onions, salt, and pepper in a bowl. Combine thoroughly.
2. In a frying pan, heat the oil over medium-low heat.
3. Make a tiny patty out of a tbsp of the potato Mixture.
4. Place the patties gently into the hot oil, and fry them up to both sides are golden brown.
5. The fritters Must be taken out of the oil and dried on paper towels.
6. Perkedel Kentang Must be served hot as a snack or side dish.

Nutrition (per serving):
Cals: ~180, Protein: ~4g, Fat: ~5g
Carbs: ~30g, Fiber: ~3g

28. Martabak Manis (Sweet Stuffed Pancake)

Prep Time: 15 mins

Cook Time: 25 mins

Total Time: 40 mins

Servings: 4

Ingredients:

- 1 cup of all-purpose flour
- 1/4 cup of granulated sugar
- 1/2 tsp baking powder
- 1/4 tsp salt
- 1 cup of milk
- 1 egg
- 1/2 tsp vanilla extract
- 2 tbsp butter, dilute
- Sweet fillings (chocolate, cheese, condensed milk, nuts, etc.)
- Butter or oil for cooking

Instructions:

1. Combine the flour, sugar, baking soda, and salt in a bowl.
2. Combine the milk, egg, vanilla essence, and dilute butter in a separate basin.
3. Blend the dry ingredients thoroughly before gradually adding the wet ingredients.
4. Add some butter or oil to a non-stick skillet that is already heated over medium heat.
5. A ladle of batter Must be poured onto the skillet and spread out to form a thin circle.
6. Sprinkle your preferred sweet fillings on one half of the pancake after cooking it up to bubbles appear on the surface.
7. To make a half-moon shape, fold the remaining half over the fillings. Cook for a few more mins or up to golden brown on both sides.
8. With the leftover batter and fillings, repeat the procedure.
9. Serve heated pancakes that have been slice into minier pieces.

Nutrition (per serving):
Cals: ~300, Protein: 7g
Carbs: 45g, Fat: 10g

29. Rendang Tahu (Tofu Rendang)

Prep Time: 20 mins

Cook Time: 40 mins

Total Time: 1 hr

Servings: 4

Ingredients:

- 1 block firm tofu, slice into cubes
- 1 can (14 oz) coconut milk
- 2 lemongrass stalks, bruised
- 3 kaffir lime leaves
- 2 tbsp oil
- 1 onion, lightly chop-up
- 3 cloves garlic, chop-up
- 1 thumb-sized ginger, chop-up
- 1 thumb-sized galangal, chop-up (non-compulsory)
- 2 tsp turmeric powder
- 1 tsp coriander powder
- 1/2 tsp cumin powder
- 1 tsp chili powder (adjust as needed)
- Salt as needed
- Sugar as needed
- Chop-up cilantro for garnish

Instructions:

1. Oil in a pot is heated to medium heat. Garlic, ginger, onion, and galangal are diced, and they are sautéed up to aromatic.
2. Add the chili powder, cumin, coriander, and turmeric powders. To blend, thoroughly stir.
3. Add the coconut milk. then cook it gently.
4. Combine the tofu cubes with the salt, sugar, lemongrass, and kaffir lime leaves. To evenly distribute the sauce, stir the tofu.
5. Stirring occasionally, et the Mixture simmer for 30 to 40 mins or up to the sauce thickens and the flavors come together.
6. Eliminate the kaffir lime and lemongrass leaves.
7. Before serving, garnish with chop-up cilantro.
8. Serve steamed rice a ongside the tofu rendang.

Nutrition (per serving):

Cals: ~280, Protein: 12g

Carbs: 14g, Fat: 20g

30. Ikan Bakar (Grilled Fish)

Prep Time: 15 mins

Cook Time: 20 mins

Total Time: 35 mins

Servings: 2

Ingredients:

- 2 whole fish (such as snapper or mackerel), cleaned and scaled
- 3 tbsp tamarind juice

- 2 tbsp oil
- 3 cloves garlic, chop-up
- 1 shallot, chop-up
- 1 tsp turmeric powder
- 1 tsp coriander powder
- 1/2 tsp cumin powder
- 1 tsp chili powder (adjust as needed)
- Salt as needed
- Banana leaves or aluminum foil for grilling
- Split limes and chop-up cilantro for garnish

Instructions:

1. To make the marinade, combine the tamarind juice, oil, chop-up gar ic, chop-up shallot, turmeric, coriander, cumin, chili powder, and salt in a bowl.
2. After scoring the fish on both sides, rub the marinade inside and out.
3. Let the fish to marinade for ten to fifteen mins.
4. Grill or grill pan before use. If using banana leaves, warm them over an open flame for a moment to make them pliable.
5. Every fish Must be wrapped in banana leaves or aluminum foil and the edges fastened.
6. The wrapped fish Must be grilled over medium heat for 15 to 20 mins, turning once or twice, or up to it is cooked through and has a smokey taste.
7. The fish Must be unwrapped and placed on serving dishes.
8. Lime slices and cilantro are garnished.
9. Along with steamed rice and your preferred dipping sauce, serve the fish on a grill.

Nutrition (per serving):

Cals: ~300, Protein: 25g

Carbs: 10g, Fat: 18g

31. Nasi Kuning (Yellow Rice)

Prep Time: 15 mins

Cook Time: 25 mins

Total Time: 40 mins

Servings: 4

Ingredients:

- 2 cups of jasmine rice
- 2 1/2 cups of coconut milk
- 1 lemongrass stalk, bruised
- 3 kaffir lime leaves
- 1 tsp turmeric powder
- 1/2 tsp salt
- 1 pandan leaf (non-compulsory)
- Fried shallots for garnish

Instructions:

1. Make sure the water flows clean when you rinse the rice in cold water. Flow freely.
2. Rice, coconut milk, lemongrass, kaffir lime leaves, turmeric powder, salt, and pandan leaf (if using) Must all be combined in a pot.
3. The components Must be thoroughly combined.
4. Stir the rice occasionally to prevent sticking while cooking it over medium heat up to the coconut milk has been absorbed and the rice is tender.
5. Take out the pandan leaf, kaffir lime leaves, and lemongrass.
6. With a fork, fluff the rice.
7. Serve the yellow rice with fried shallots as a garnish.

Nutrition (per serving):

Cals: ~350, Protein: 5g

Carbs: 60g, Fat: 10g

32. Nasi Campur (Combined Rice Dish)

Prep Time: 30 mins

Cook Time: 40 mins

Total Time: 1 hr 10 mins

Servings: 4

Ingredients:

- 2 cups of cooked white rice
- 200g grilled chicken, split
- 200g beef rendang, shredded
- 1 cup of sambal (chili paste)
- 4 eggs, hard-boiled and halved
- 1 cup of stir-fried vegetables (long beans, cabbage, carrots)
- 1 cucumber, split
- 1 cup of krupuk (shrimp crackers)
- Fried shallots for garnish

Instructions:

1. A bit of cooked rice Must be placed on a dish.
2. Over the rice, scatter the grilled chicken in slices and the beef rendang in shreds.
3. Place a spoonful of sambal on the plate's side.
4. Put the hard-boiled eggs in halves on the platter.
5. Include the cucumber slices and the stir-fried vegetables.
6. Garnish with fried shallots and serve with krupuk on the side.
7. For every serving, repeat.

33. Sambal Goreng Kentang (Spicy Fried Potatoes)

Prep Time: 15 mins

Cook Time: 20 mins

Total Time: 35 mins

Servings: 4

Ingredients:

- 4 medium potatoes, peel off and slice into thin strips
- 1 onion, lightly split
- 3 cloves garlic, chop-up
- 2 red chilies, split
- 1 tsp shrimp paste (terasi)
- 1 tsp tamarind paste
- 1 tsp sugar
- Salt as needed
- Cooking oil for frying

Instructions:

1. Fry the potato strips in hot frying oil up to they are brown and crispy. Take out, then dry off with paper towels.
2. Heat some oil in a different skillet and cook the onion and garlic up to they are fragrant.
3. Continue sautéing after adding the shrimp paste and thinly chop-up red chilies.
4. Add salt, sugar, and tamarind paste after combining. Combine thoroughly.
5. Toss the cooked potato strips in the hot Mixture after adding them to the pan.
6. Cook for a few more mins to really meld the flavors.
7. As a side dish, serve warm.

34. Papeda (Papuan Sago Porridge)

Prep Time: 5 mins

Cook Time: 15 mins

Total Time: 20 mins

Servings: 2

Ingredients:

- 1 cup of sago pearls
- 4 cups of water
- Salt as needed

Instructions:

1. Bring the water to a boil in a pot.
2. Sago pearls Must be added gradually while being regularly stirred to avoid clumping.
3. The liquid will thicken and become translucent after about 10-15 mins of stirring and cooking.
4. As needed, add salt to the dish.

5. Before serving, take it off the fire and let it cool somewhat.

35. Bubur Ayam (Chicken Congee)

Prep Time: 10 mins

Cook Time: 1 hr

Total Time: 1 hr 10 mins

Servings: 4

Ingredients:

- 1 cup of rice
- 4 cups of chicken broth
- 200g cooked chicken, shredded
- 2 eggs, beaten and cooked into thin omelets, then split
- Fried shallots for garnish
- Split spring onions for garnish
- Salt and pepper as needed

Instructions:

1. Drain the rice after giving it a good rinse.
2. Rice Must be added to a pot along with the boiling chicken broth.
3. Rice Must boil over low heat for a while, stirring occasionally, up to it thickens into a porridge.
4. Cook for an additional 10 to 15 mins before adding the chicken shreds.
5. Add salt and pepper as needed.
6. Congee Must be served hot with split omelets, fried shallots, and thinly split spring onions on top.

36. Sate Kambing (Lamb Satay)

Prep Time: 20 mins

Cook Time: 15 mins

Total Time: 35 mins

Servings: 4

Ingredients:

- 1 lb (450g) lamb meat, slice into thin strips
- 1 tbsp vegetable oil
- Wooden skewers, soaked in water
- Salt and pepper as needed
- For the Marinade:
- 2 cloves garlic, chop-up
- 1 shallot, chop-up
- 1 tsp turmeric powder
- 1 tsp cumin powder
- 1 tsp coriander powder
- 2 tbsp soy sauce
- 2 tbsp kecap manis (sweet soy sauce)

Instructions:

1. Combine all the marinade ingredients in a bowl.

2. Make sure the lamb strips are thoroughly covered in the marinade before adding them. For at least an hr, cover and marinate.
3. Onto the prepared skewers, thread the marinated lamb strips.
4. A grill or grill pan Must be preheated to high heat. Use vegetable oil to brush.
5. The lamb satay Must be prepared to your preferred doneness by grilling it for two to three mins on every side.
6. As needed, add salt and pepper to the food.
7. Rice and peanut sauce Must be served with the lamb satay.

37. Sop Bening (Clear Vegetable Soup)

Prep Time: 15 mins

Cook Time: 20 mins

Total Time: 35 mins

Servings: 4

Ingredients:

- 4 cups of vegetable broth
- 1 carrot, split
- 1 cup of green beans, slice into bite-sized pieces
- 1 cup of corn kernels
- 1 cup of cabbage, shredded
- 1 tomato, split
- 2 cloves garlic, chop-up
- 1 tsp ginger, chop-up
- Salt and pepper as needed
- Chop-up cilantro for garnish

Instructions:

1. Garlic and ginger that has been chop-up Must be cooked in a mini amount of oil up to aromatic.
2. Bring the vegetable broth to a boil after adding it.
3. Adding the carrot slices, simmer for a few mins, or up to they start to soften.
4. Green beans, maize, cabbage, and tomato Must be added. Simmer a l of the vegetables up to they are ready.
5. As needed, add salt and pepper to the food.
6. Before serving, garnish with chop-up cilantro.

39. Rendang Telur (Egg Rendang)

Prep Time: 10 mins

Cook Time: 40 mins

Total Time: 50 mins

Servings: 4

Ingredients:

- 6 hard-boiled eggs, peel off
- 1 can coconut milk (14 oz)
- 2 kaffir lime leaves

- 1 lemongrass stalk, bruised
- 1 cinnamon stick
- 2 star anise
- 3 tbsp rendang curry paste
- Salt as needed
- Chop-up cilantro for garnish

Instructions:

1. Coconut milk, kaffir lime leaves, lemongrass, cinnamon stick, star anise, and rendang curry paste Must all be combined in a pot. Bring to a simmering boil.
2. To the pot, add the hard-boiled eggs.
3. For 30 to 40 mins, simmer the eggs in the coconut milk Mixture, stirring occasionally, up to the sauce has thickened and is coating the eggs.
4. As needed, add salt to the dish.
5. Before serving, garnish with chop-up cilantro.

40. Tahu Gejrot (Fried Tofu with Spicy Sauce)

Prep Time: 15 mins

Cook Time: 10 mins

Total Time: 25 mins

Servings: 4

Ingredients:

- 8 mini firm tofu blocks, fried and slice into bite-sized pieces
- 3 shallots, thinly split
- 2 red chilies, thinly split
- 2 cloves garlic, chop-up
- 2 tbsp sweet soy sauce (kecap manis)
- 1 tbsp soy sauce
- 1 tsp tamarind paste
- Salt and sugar as needed
- For the Spicy Sauce:
- 3 shallots, chop-up
- 2 red chilies, chop-up
- 2 cloves garlic, chop-up
- 1 tbsp vegetable oil
- 1 tsp shrimp paste (non-compulsory)
- 1 tsp sugar

Instructions:

1. The sauce is made by combining the sweet soy sauce, soy sauce, tamarind paste, salt, and sugar in a bowl.
2. Chop-up shallots, red chilies, and garlic Must be sautéed in a pan up to aromatic.
3. Stir thoroughly after adding the sauce Mixture to the pan.
4. Toss the fried tofu pieces in the sauce in the pan after adding them. Cook for a little while.

5. Sauté the chop-up shallots, red chilies, and garlic in oil up to fragrant to make the hot sauce. Stir well after adding the sugar and shrimp paste (if using).
6. Serve the spicy sauce on the side with the fried tofu.

41. Klepon (Sweet Rice Cake with Palm Sugar)

Prep Time: 30 mins

Cook Time: 30 mins

Total Time: 1 hr

Servings: Makes about 20 pieces

Ingredients:

- 2 cups of glutinous rice flour
- 1 cup of finely grated coconut (for coating)
- 200g palm sugar, slice into mini cubes
- A pinch of salt
- Green food coloring (non-compulsory)
- Pandan leaves (for aroma)

Instructions:

1. Combine the glutinous rice flour with a dash of salt in a combining dish. As you knead the dough, add water gradually to create a smooth dough.
2. In your palm, press little pieces of dough into the surface. Wrap the dough around a cube of palm sugar in the center, creating a ball.
3. Bring water in a big pot to a boil. Add a few drops of green food coloring, if desired, and the pandan leaves for aroma.
4. Enter the boiling water with the rice balls. Once cooked (typically in 3–4 mins), they will float to the top after initially sinking to the bottom.
5. After removing the cooked rice balls from the pot with a slotted spoon, immediately coat them with finely grated coconut.
6. Before serving, let them to cool just a little. A sweet filling will be produced when the palm sugar melts.

Nutrition (per serving):

Cals: 120 kcal, Carbs: 25g, Fat: 2g

Protein: 1g, Fiber: 1g

42. Tumis Kangkung (Stir-fried Water Spinach)

Prep Time: 15 mins

Cook Time: 10 mins

Total Time: 25 mins

Servings: 4

Ingredients:

- 1 bunch of water spinach (kangkung), washed and slice into 2-inch pieces
- 2 cloves garlic, chop-up
- 2 shallots, thinly split
- 2 red chili peppers, split (adjust as needed)
- 1 tbsp cooking oil
- 1 tsp shrimp paste (terasi), non-compulsory
- Salt and sugar as needed

Instructions:

1. Over medium heat, warm the cooking oil in the pan. Sauté the shallots in their slices and chop-up garlic up to aromatic.
2. If you're using shrimp paste, put some in the pan and stir-fry it for a min to let the flavor come out.
3. Stir-fry for an additional min after adding the thinly split chile peppers.
4. Stir-fry the water spinach that has been added to the pan up to it wilts and becomes cooked but still has a tiny crunch.
5. As needed, add a little sugar and salt to the food. Combine thoroughly.
6. Transfer to a serving dish after taking it off the heat.

Nutrition (per serving):
Cals: 45 kcal, Carbs: 7g, Fat: 2g

Protein: 2g, Fiber: 2g

43. Serabi (Coconut Pancakes)

Prep Time: 10 mins

Cook Time: 15 mins

Total Time: 25 mins

Servings: Makes about 10 pancakes

Ingredients:

- 1 cup of rice flour
- 1/2 cup of all-purpose flour
- 1 cup of coconut milk
- 1/2 cup of water
- 1/4 cup of granulated sugar
- 1/4 tsp salt
- Banana leaves or parchment paper (for lining)
- Finely grated coconut and palm sugar syrup (gula aren) for topping

Instructions:

1. Rice flour, all-purpose flour, sugar, and salt Must all be combined in a bowl.
2. To get a smooth batter, gradually whisk in the water and coconut milk.
3. A nonstick pan Must be heated to medium. Put some parchment paper or a banana leaf on the pan.

4. To create a little pancake, spoon some batter onto the leaf or piece of paper.
5. Flip the pancake over and continue cooking it up to both sides are golden brown after little bubbles start to develop on the surface.
6. With the remaining batter, repeat the procedure.
7. Serve the serabi with finely grated coconut on top and some palm sugar syrup drizzled over it.

Nutrition (per serving, without toppings):
Cals: 120 kcal, Carbs: 25g

Fat: 1g, Protein: 2g, Fiber: 1g

44.Sayur Asem (Tamarind Vegetable Soup)

Prep Time: 20 mins

Cook Time: 30 mins

Total Time: 50 mins

Servings: 6

Ingredients:

- 4 cups of water
- 100g snake beans or green beans, slice into 2-inch pieces
- 1 mini eggplant, slice into chunks
- 1 tomato, quartered
- 100g corn kernels
- 2 pieces of Indonesian bay leaves (daun salam)
- 2 kaffir lime leaves
- 1 lemongrass stalk, bruised
- 1 tsp tamarind paste
- 1 tsp palm sugar or brown sugar
- Salt as needed

Instructions:

1. Bring the water to a boil in a pot. Add the corn kernels, tomato, eggplant, and snake beans.
2. Add the lemongrass, kaffir lime leaves, and Indonesian bay leaves.
3. Put a little water and the tamarind paste in a mini bowl, and then drain the juice into a pot.
4. Add salt and palm sugar. Simmer the soup for a while to let the vegetables soften.
5. If necessary, adjust the seasoning.
6. With hot rice, serve the soup.

Nutrition (per serving):
Cals: 60 kcal, Carbs: 15g, Fat: 0g

Protein: 1g, Fiber: 3g

45.Sate Lilit (Balinese Chop-up Satay)

Prep Time: 30 mins

Cook Time: 15 mins

Total Time: 45 mins

Servings: 4

Ingredients:

- 300g chop-up chicken or fish
- 2 shallots, lightly chop-up
- 2 cloves garlic, chop-up
- 2 red chillies, deseeded and chop-up
- 1 tsp shrimp paste (terasi)
- 1 tsp turmeric powder
- 1 tsp cumin powder
- 1 tsp coriander powder
- 1 tsp palm sugar or brown sugar
- Salt as needed
- Lemongrass stalks, for skewers

Instructions:

1. Combine the chop-up chicken or fish, shallots, garlic, red pepper flakes, shrimp paste, turmeric, cumin, coriander, palm sugar, and salt in a bowl. Blend thoroughly.
2. To construct a cylindrical shape, take little amounts of the Mixture and wrap the lemongrass stalks in them.
3. Cook the skewers on a grill or grill pan for 10-15 mins, or up to they are thoroughly heated through and gently browned.
4. The Sate Lilit Must be served hot with steamed rice and your preferred dipping sauce.

46.Pindang Ikan (Spiced Fish Stew)

Prep Time: 20 mins

Cook Time: 40 mins

Total Time: 1 hr

Servings: 6

Ingredients:

- 600g fish fillets (snapper, mackerel, or any firm white fish), slice into chunks
- 2 tomatoes, split
- 2 lemongrass stalks, bruised
- 3 kaffir lime leaves
- 4 shallots, split
- 3 cloves garlic, chop-up
- 2 red chillies, split
- 1 tsp tamarind paste
- 1 tsp palm sugar or brown sugar
- 1 tsp salt
- 500ml water
- Banana leaves for wrapping (non-compulsory)

Instructions:

1. Water, shallots, garlic, red pepper flakes, lemongrass, kaffir lime leaves, tamarind paste,

palm sugar, and salt Must all be combined in a pot. up to a boil.
2. To the pot, add the tomato slices and fish chunks. Up to the flavors combine and the fish is cooked through, lower the heat and let the stew simmer for about 30 to 40 mins.
3. If using banana leaves, pass them quickly over an open flame to make them pliable. A portion of the stew Must be placed on a banana leaf and neatly box/pkgd.
4. Serve steamed rice beside the pindang ikan.

47. Dadar Gulung (Pandan Crepes)

Prep Time: 15 mins

Cook Time: 15 mins

Total Time: 30 mins

Servings: 4

Ingredients:

- 1 cup of all-purpose flour
- 2 eggs
- 1 ½ cups of coconut milk
- ½ cup of pandan juice (extract from pandan leaves)
- ¼ tsp salt
- ½ cup of granulated sugar
- Finely grated coconut, for filling

Instructions:

1. All-purpose flour, eggs, coconut milk, pandan juice, salt, and the other half of the sugar Must be whipped together into a homogeneous batter in a basin.
2. A nonstick pan Must be heated to medium. A mini ladleful of the batter Must be poured into the pan, and it Must be swirled to uniformly coat the bottom. Once the crepe is set, fry it for an additional 1–2 mins on the opposite side. Continue by using the remaining batter.
3. Combine the finely grated coconut and the remaining sugar to make the filling.
4. Every crepe Must have a tsp of the finely grated coconut that has been sweetened. Then, fold the sides to form a roll.
5. The Dadar Gulung is delicious as a dessert or a snack.

48.Mie Aceh (Spicy Acehnese Noodles)

Prep Time: 20 mins

Cook Time: 40 mins

Total Time: 1 hr

Servings: 4

Ingredients:

- 250g egg noodles
- 200g chicken, split
- 150g shrimp, peel off and deveined
- 2 tomatoes, diced
- 3 cloves garlic, chop-up
- 2 shallots, chop-up
- 2 red chillies, split
- 1 tsp turmeric powder
- 1 tsp cumin powder
- 1 tsp coriander powder
- 1 stalk lemongrass, bruised
- 2 kaffir lime leaves
- 500ml chicken broth
- 200ml coconut milk
- 2 tbsp vegetable oil
- Salt and pepper as needed
- Lime wedges and fried shallots for garnish

Instructions:

1. Follow the directions on the box/pkg to boil the egg noodles. Drain, then set apart.
2. Garlic, shallots, and red peppers Must be sautéed in hot vegetable oil up to aromatic.
3. Cook the chicken and shrimp after adding them up to they begin to get opaque.
4. Add the powdered turmeric, cumin, and coriander.
5. Add the lemongrass and kaffir lime leaves after adding the chicken broth. Simmer the broth for 15 to 20 mins.
6. Add the coconut milk and diced tomatoes. Add salt and pepper as needed. Ten more mins of simmering.
7. Pour the hot soup over a portion of the cooked noodles in a bowl to serve.
8. Lime wedges and fried shallots are garnishes.

49.Karedok (Raw Vegetable Salad with Peanut Sauce)

Prep Time: 20 mins

Cook Time: 0 mins

Total Time: 20 mins

Servings: 4

Ingredients:

- 2 cups of bean sprouts
- 1 cup of cucumber, julienned
- 1 cup of string beans, slice into 2-inch pieces and blanched
- 1 cup of cabbage, lightly shredded
- 1 cup of water spinach (kangkung), blanched and chop-up
- 2 cloves garlic

- 3-4 bird's eye chilies (adjust as needed)
- 1 cup of roasted peanuts
- 1 tbsp tamarind paste
- 1 tbsp palm sugar or brown sugar
- Salt as needed
- Water
- Shrimp crackers (non-compulsory)

Instructions:

1. To make the peanut sauce, mash together the garlic, chilies, roasted peanuts, tamarind paste, palm sugar, and a dash of salt in a mortar and pestle. To achieve the correct consistency, add water as necessary.
2. Bean sprouts, cucumber, string beans, cabbage, and water spinach Must all be combined in a sizable combining basin.
3. Give the vegetables a good coating of peanut sauce after pouring it over them.
4. If desired, top the salad with shrimp crackers before serving.

Nutrition (per serving):

Cals: ~250 kcal, Protein: ~10g

Carbs: ~15g

Fat: ~18g, Fiber: ~4g

50. Cumi Goreng Tepung (Fried Calamari)

Prep Time: 15 mins

Cook Time: 15 mins

Total Time: 30 mins

Servings: 4

Ingredients:

- 1 lb calamari, cleaned and slice into rings
- 1 cup of all-purpose flour
- 1 tsp salt
- 1/2 tsp ground black pepper
- 1 tsp garlic powder
- 1 tsp paprika
- Oil for frying
- Lemon wedges for serving

Instructions:

1. Combine the flour, salt, black pepper, paprika, and garlic powder in a bowl.
2. 350°F (175°C) oil temperature in a deep frying pan or pot.
3. Shake off any excess flour Mixture before coating the calamari rings.
4. Fry the calamari in batches for 2 to 3 mins per batch, or up to golden brown and crispy. Never overfill the pan.
5. With a slotted spoon, take out the deep-fried

calamari and set them on a plate covered in paper towels to absorb any remaining oil.

6. With lemon slices, serve hot.

Nutrition (per serving, including frying oil):
Cals: ~300 kcal, Protein: ~20g, Carbs: ~30g

Fat: ~10g, Fiber: ~1g

51. Ayam Goreng Kalasan (Kalasan Fried Chicken)

Prep Time: 4 hrs (marination time included)

Cook Time: 30 mins

Total Time: 4 hrs 30 mins

Servings: 4

Ingredients:
- 4 chicken legs and thighs, skin-on
- 3 shallots, roughly chop-up
- 2 cloves garlic, roughly chop-up
- 1 tsp coriander seeds
- 1 tsp turmeric powder
- 1 tbsp palm sugar or brown sugar
- 1 tsp salt
- 1 tbsp tamarind juice
- 1 tbsp coconut oil
- Banana leaves for wrapping (non-compulsory)
- Cooking oil for frying

Instructions:
1. Shallots, garlic, coriander seeds, turmeric powder, palm sugar, salt, tamarind juice, and coconut oil Must be blended into a paste in a blender.
2. For better taste, leave the chicken in the paste overnight or at least for four hrs.
3. If using banana leaves, slice them into squares and warm them over an open flame for a few seconds to make them pliable.
4. Every piece of marinated chicken Must be wrapped in a banana leaf and fastened with toothpicks.
5. Fry the chicken in a pan with hot oil for about 15 mins per side, or up to it is golden brown and thoroughly cooked.
6. With steamed rice, serve the fried chicken.

Nutrition (per serving, including frying oil):
Cals: ~400 kcal, Protein: ~25g, Carbs: ~10g

Fat: ~30g, Fiber: ~1g

52. Pepes Udang (Steamed Shrimp in Banana Leaves)

Prep Time: 30 mins

Cook Time: 30 mins

Total Time: 1 hr

Servings: 4

Ingredients:
- 1 lb Big shrimp, peel off and deveined
- 2 shallots, lightly split
- 2 cloves garlic, chop-up
- 1 tsp turmeric powder
- 1 tsp ground coriander
- 1 tsp ground cumin
- 1 tsp palm sugar or brown sugar
- 1 tsp salt
- 2 kaffir lime leaves, thinly split
- 2 red chilies, thinly split
- Banana leaves for wrapping
- Toothpicks or kitchen twine

Instructions:
1. The shrimp, shallots, garlic, turmeric powder, ground cumin, ground coriander, palm sugar, salt, kaffir lime leaves, and red chilies Must all be combined in a bowl. Combine together and let sit for 15 to 20 mins to marinate.
2. Banana leaves Must be slice up into squares and melted by briefly heating them over an open flame.
3. Every square of the banana leaf Must have some of the shrimp Mixture that has been marinated. The leaves Must then be folded to form a packet. To keep the sachets closed, use kitchen twine or toothpicks.
4. To cook the shrimp, steam the banana leaf box/pkgs for 20 to 25 mins.
5. Steamed rice Must be served alongside the shrimp packets.

Nutrition (per serving):
Cals: ~150 kcal, Protein: ~20g, Carbs: ~6g

Fat: ~5g, Fiber: ~1g

53. Es Doger (Coconut Milk Ice Dessert)

Prep Time: 15 mins

Cook Time: 15 mins

Total Time: 30 mins

Servings: 4

Ingredients:
- 2 cups of coconut milk
- 1/2 cup of palm sugar, finely grated
- 1/4 cup of condensed milk

- 1/4 cup of jackfruit, diced
- 1/4 cup of sweet potatoes, boiled and diced
- 1/4 cup of young coconut meat, shredded
- 1/4 cup of coconut meatballs (from the center of the coconut)
- 1/4 cup of diced bread
- 1/4 cup of crushed ice
- 1/4 tsp salt
- 1/4 tsp vanilla extract
- 1/4 tsp pink food coloring (non-compulsory)

Instructions:

1. Combine coconut milk and palm sugar in a pot. Cook the sugar up to it dissolves over medium heat. Observe cooling.
2. The coconut milk combination Must be combined with condensed milk, vanilla essence, and salt. Stir thoroughly, then chill.
3. Layer the chop-up jackfruit, sweet potatoes, flesh from a young coconut, coconut meatballs, and bread in serving glasses.
4. In the glasses, add the cooled coconut milk Mixture on top.
5. Add a few drops of pink food coloring, if desired, and some crushed ice on top.
6. Serve the reviving Es Doger right away and savor it!

Nutrition (per serving):

Cals: 320, Fat: 18g

Carbs: 38g

Protein: 4g, Fiber: 2g

54. Bebek Goreng (Crispy Fried Duck)

Prep Time: 1 hr

Cook Time: 45 mins

Total Time: 1 hr 45 mins

Servings: 4

Ingredients:

- 1 whole duck, cleaned and slice into serving pieces
- 2 tbsp turmeric powder
- 1 tbsp coriander powder
- 1 tsp salt
- 1 tsp pepper
- 4 kaffir lime leaves, lightly chop-up
- Oil for deep frying

Instructions:

1. To make a marinade, combine the salt, pepper, turmeric, coriander, and chop-up kaffir lime leaves in a basin.

2. Make sure the duck pieces are evenly covered by rubbing the marinade all over them. Give it at least one hr to marinate.
3. A deep frying pan with medium-high heat is used to heat the oil.
4. Duck pieces Must be carefully added to the heated oil and fried up to golden and crispy.
5. To drain off extra oil, take out the fried duck pieces from the oil and place them on paper towels.
6. Along with steaming rice and sambal (chili sauce), serve the Bebek Goreng hot.

Nutrition (per serving):

Cals: 450, Fat: 30g

Carbs: 2g

Protein: 40g, Fiber: 1g

55. Pecel (Javanese Salad with Peanut Sauce)

Prep Time 20 mins

Cook Time: 10 mins

Total Time: 30 mins

Servings: 4

Ingredients:

- 4 cups of combined vegetables (cabbage, bean sprouts, water spinach, cucumber), blanched
- 1 cup of rice vermicelli, cooked according to box/pkg instructions
- 1 cup of mung bean sprouts
- 1 cup of tofu, fried and split
- 1 cup of tempeh, fried and split
- 1 cup of krupuk (shrimp crackers)
- 1/2 cup of peanuts, roasted and ground
- 2 cloves garlic
- 3-4 red chili peppers (adjust as needed)
- 2 tbsp tamarind juice
- 1 tbsp palm sugar
- Salt as needed
- Water as needed

Instructions:

1. Make a paste out of garlic, red chili peppers, and a little salt in a mortar and pestle.
2. Combine the ground peanuts, tamarind juice, palm sugar, and chili-garlic paste in a mini bowl. To achieve a sauce-like consistency, add water. If necessary, adjust flavors by using extra tamarind, sugar, or salt.
3. On a serving plate, arrange the blanched vegetables, rice vermicelli, bean sprouts, tofu, tempeh, and krupuk.

4. Sprinkle the assembled items with the peanut sauce.
5. Serve the Pecel right away, combining the ingredients and sauce before consuming.

Nutrition (per serving):
Cals: 350, Fat: 15g

Carbs: 45g

Protein: 15g, Fiber: 8g

56 Soto Madura (Madurese Beef Soup)

Prep Time: 20 mins

Cook Time: 2 hrs

Total Time: 2 hrs 20 mins

Servings: 6

Ingredients:
- 1 lb beef, slice into bite-sized pieces
- 6 cups of water
- 2 lemongrass stalks, bruised
- 4 kaffir lime leaves
- 2 bay leaves
- 2 tsp ground coriander
- 1 tsp ground turmeric
- Salt and pepper as needed
- 1 tbsp oil
- Rice vermicelli, cooked according to box/pkg instructions
- Bean sprouts, lime wedges, fried shallots, and chop-up cilantro for serving

Instructions:
1. Ground coriander and ground turmeric Must be sautéed in oil over medium heat up to aromatic.
2. Cook the beef after adding it up to the color changes.
3. Add water, bay leaves, lemongrass, and kaffir lime leaves. When the beef is tender, simmer for about 2 hrs with the heat reduced after bringing the Mixture to a boil.
4. As needed, add salt and pepper to the food.
5. When ready to serve, put cooked rice vermicelli in dishes and add cooked beef and broth on top.
6. Bean sprouts, lime wedges, fried shallots, and chop-up cilantro are garnishing options.
7. Serve the Soto Madura hot with extra toppings on the side, such as sambal and kecap manis (sweet soy sauce).

Nutrition (per serving):
Cals: 300, Fat: 15g, Carbs: 20g, Protein: 25g
Fiber: 2g

57.Es Campur (Combined Ice Dessert)

Prep Time: 20 mins

Cook Time: 0 mins

Total Time: 20 mins

Servings: 4

Ingredients:
- 1 cup of shaved ice
- Assorted fruits (such as jackfruit, coconut, avocado, etc.), diced
- 1/2 cup of sweetened condensed milk
- 1/4 cup of rose syrup
- 1/4 cup of coconut milk
- 1/4 cup of grass jelly, cubed
- 1/4 cup of palm sugar syrup
- 1 tbsp agar jelly, slice into mini cubes
- 1 tbsp tapioca pearls, cooked

Instructions:
1. Slice the fruits into bite-sized pieces to prepare all the ingredients.
2. A layer of shaved ice Must be placed in serving bowls or glasses.
3. Over the ice, scatter a variety of diced fruits.
4. Over the fruits, drizzle coconut milk, rose syrup, and sweetened condensed milk.
5. The bowls Must now contain grass jelly and agar jelly cubes.
6. Add some cooked tapioca pearls and a tsp of palm sugar syrup on top.
7. Serve the dessert of blended ice right away and savor its cooling flavor!

Nutrition (per serving):
Cals: Approximately 250 kcal, Carbs: 50g
Sugars: 30g, Fat: 5g, Protein: 2g, Fiber: 2g

58. Nasi Liwet (Coconut Rice with Chicken and Vegetables)

Prep Time: 30 mins

Cook Time: 40 mins

Total Time: 1 hr 10 mins

Servings: 4

Ingredients:
- 2 cups of jasmine rice
- 1 cup of coconut milk
- 2 cups of water
- 2 lemongrass stalks, bruised
- 4 kaffir lime leaves
- 1 tsp salt
- 1 tsp sugar
- 8 pieces chicken pieces (thighs and drumsticks)
- 2 cloves garlic, chop-up
- 1 tsp turmeric powder
- 1 cup of green beans, slice into 2-inch pieces
- 1 cup of carrots, julienned

- Fried shallots for garnish
- Split cucumber for garnish

Instructions:

1. Drain the rice after giving it a good rinse.
2. Rice, coconut milk, water, lemongrass, kaffir lime leaves, salt, and sugar Must all be combined in a saucepan. Rice Must be prepared as you normally would.
3. For around 15 mins, season the chicken pieces with salt, pepper, turmeric powder, and chop-up garlic.
4. Cooking and lightly browning the marinated chicken in a separate skillet with hot oil. Place aside.
5. Green beans and carrots Must be stir-fried in the same pan up to they are cooked. Add a little salt for flavor.
6. Serve the chicken and stir-fried vegetables with the cooked coconut rice.
7. Add cucumber slices and fried shallots as a garnish.
8. Take pleasure in your tasty Nasi Liwet!

Nutrition (per serving):

Cals: Approximately 500 kcal, Carbs: 60g

Protein: 20g, Fat: 20g, Fiber: 4g

59. Opor Ayam (Chicken in Coconut Milk)

Prep Time: 15 mins

Cook Time: 45 mins

Total Time: 1 hr

Servings: 6

Ingredients:

- 1 whole chicken, slice into pieces
- 2 tbsp vegetable oil
- 2 onions, lightly chop-up
- 3 cloves garlic, chop-up
- 1 tsp ginger paste
- 1 tsp galangal paste (non-compulsory)
- 1 tsp turmeric powder
- 1 tsp coriander powder
- 1/2 tsp white pepper
- 4 kaffir lime leaves
- 2 lemongrass stalks, bruised
- 2 cups of coconut milk
- 1 cup of chicken broth
- Salt, as needed
- Palm sugar or brown sugar, as needed
- Hard-boiled eggs (non-compulsory), peel off
- Fried shallots for garnish

Instructions:

1. The chop-up onions, chop-up garlic, ginger paste, and galangal paste Must be sautéed in hot vegetable oil up to aromatic.
2. White pepper, coriander, and turmeric powders Must be added. Stir thoroughly.
3. Cook the chicken chunks after adding them up to they begin to brown.
4. Add the chicken broth and coconut milk. Add lemongrass and kaffir lime leaves.
5. Cook the chicken for 30 to 40 mins, or up to it is cooked, at a simmer.
6. To obtain the required flavor harmony, season the dish with salt and palm sugar.
7. If using, add the hard-boiled eggs to the pot and cook them for a few mins so they can absorb the flavors.
8. Over steaming rice, top the Opor Ayam with fried shallots as a garnish.
9. Enjoy this mouthwatering coconut milk and chicken dish!

Nutrition (per serving):

Cals: Approximately 400 kcal, Carbs: 9g

Protein: 20g, Fat: 32g, Fiber: 1g

60. Pempek Kapal Selam (Submarine Fishcake)

Prep Time: 30 mins

Cook Time: 30 mins

Total Time: 1 hr

Servings: 4

Ingredients:

For Fishcake:

- 500g ground fish (mackerel or other white fish)
- 150g tapioca starch
- 2 cloves garlic, chop-up
- 1 tsp salt
- 1/2 tsp white pepper
- 150ml ice water
- For Filling:
- 4 hard-boiled eggs, peel off

For Sauce:

- 200ml vinegar
- 100g palm sugar
- 1 tsp salt
- 3 cloves garlic, chop-up
- 3 red chili peppers, chop-up (adjust as needed)
- 1/2 tsp shrimp paste (non-compulsory)

Instructions:

1. For the fishcake, combine the ground fish,

tapioca starch, chop-up garlic, salt, and white pepper in a big bowl.

2. As you continue to combine, gradually add ice water, and continue up to the Mixture is smooth and elastic.
3. A hard-boiled egg Must be placed in the center of a tiny amount of the fish Mixture that has been flattened in your palm. The Mixture Must then be wrapped around the egg.
4. Repeat with the remaining fish and eggs.
5. When cooking:
6. Put some water on to boil. The fishcake-filled eggs Must be carefully added, and they Must cook up to they float to the top, signaling that they are done.
7. The cooked fishcakes Must be take outd and leted to cool.
8. For the sauce, combine the salt, vinegar, and palm sugar in a saucepan. Cook the sugar up to it melts.
9. Add shrimp paste, chop-up garlic, and chop-up red chili peppers. Cook for a short while to let the flavors blend.
10. The sauce Must cool.
11. Slice the fishcake-stuffed eggs into halves or quarters to serve.
12. Drizzle the sauce over the Pempek Kapal Selam before serving.
13. If you'd like, you may also add more chop-up cucumbers and fried shallots to the dish.
14. Enjoy this delicious and distinctive Indonesian meal.

Nutrition (per serving):
Cals: Approximately 300 kcal, Carbs: 30g

Protein: 20g, Fat: 10g, Fiber: 1g

61.Rujak Cingur (Surabaya Combined Salad)

Prep Time: 30 mins

Cook Time: 15 mins

Total Time: 45 mins

Servings: 4

Ingredients:
- 200g beef snout (cingur), boiled and split
- 200g cucumber, julienned
- 150g raw bean sprouts
- 150g pineapple, thinly split
- 100g fried tofu, cubed
- 100g fried tempeh, split
- 100g water spinach (kangkung), blanched
- 3 red chilies, split
- 3 cloves garlic

- 2 tbsp palm sugar
- 2 tbsp tamarind juice
- 1 tbsp shrimp paste (terasi), roasted
- 1 tbsp fried shallots
- Salt as needed

Instructions:
1. Grind the red chilies, garlic, shrimp paste, palm sugar, and salt together to make the spicy seasoning.
2. Combine the tamarind juice, hot spice, and beef snout slices. Give it some time to marinade.
3. Place the fried tofu, fried tempeh, pineapple, julienned cucumber, bean sprouts, and water spinach on a serving platter.
4. Top the vegetables with the beef snout that has been marinated.
5. Pour the tamarind juice over the beef and vegetables.
6. Add fried shallots as a garnish.
7. Serve the rujak cingur with lontong or rice cakes.

NUTRITION INFO: (per serving, approximate)
Cals: 320, Protein: 14g

Fat: 18g, Carbs: 28g, Fiber: 4g

62.Sambal Goreng Tempeh (Spicy Tempeh Stir-fry)

Prep Time: 15 mins

Cook Time: 20 mins

Total Time: 35 mins

Servings: 4

Ingredients:
- 2 cups of tempeh, cubed
- 1 onion, thinly split
- 3 cloves garlic, chop-up
- 2 red chili peppers, split
- 2 tbsp vegetable oil
- 1 tsp shrimp paste (non-compulsory)
- 2 tbsp sweet soy sauce (kecap manis)
- 1 tsp tamarind paste
- Salt as needed
- Sugar as needed
- Water for boiling tempeh

Instructions:
1. Ten mins Must be allotted for boiling the diced tempeh. Drain, then set apart.
2. In a pan, heat the vegetable oil on medium. Include the chop-up garlic, onion, and chili peppers. up to fragrant, sauté.
3. Stir-fry the boiling tempeh for a few mins up to it begins to brown after being added to the pan.

4. If using shrimp paste, pour it in and give it a good toss.
5. Add the tamarind paste and sweet soy sauce. Combine just enough to evenly coat the tempeh.
6. As needed, add salt and sugar to the dish. You can adjust the sweetness and heat to your liking.
7. Stir-fry the tempeh for a further 5-7 mins to achieve a crispy, well-cooked texture.
8. Steamed rice Must be served with the sambal goreng tempeh.

NUTRITION INFO: (Per Serving, approximate)
Cals: 250 kcal, Protein: 15g
Carbs: 15g, Fat: 15g, Fiber: 3g

63. Bubur Ketan Hitam (Black Glutinous Rice Porridge)

Prep Time: 8 hrs (for soaking rice)
Cook Time: 1 hr
Total Time: 9 hrs
Servings: 6

Ingredients:
- 1 cup of black glutinous rice, soaked overnight
- 5 cups of water
- 1 pandan leaf (screwpine leaf), tied in a knot
- 1 cup of coconut milk
- 1/2 cup of palm sugar (gula aren), or as needed
- Pinch of salt
- Coconut cream, for topping

Instructions:
1. Rinse the black glutinous rice in cold water up to the water is clear after it has been soaked.
2. The soaked rice, water, and pandan leaf Must all be combined in a pot. Bring to a boil, then lower the heat to a simmer, stirring regularly, for 45 to 60 mins, or up to the rice is soft and the Mixture has thickened.
3. To the pot, add a tsp of salt, the palm sugar, and the coconut milk. Cook for a further 10 to 15 mins after a thorough stirring.
4. Take the pandan leaf off.
5. Serve the hot bubur ketan hitam with a dollop of coconut cream on top.

NUTRITION INFO: (Per Serving, approximate)
Cals: 250 kcal, Protein: 3g, Carbs: 55g
Fat: 4g, Fiber: 2g

64. Bakso (Indonesian Meatballs)

Prep Time: 30 mins
Cook Time: 30 mins
Total Time: 1 hr
Servings: 4

Ingredients:
- 300g ground beef or chicken
- 100g tapioca flour or cornstarch
- 1 egg
- 2 cloves garlic, chop-up
- 1 tsp salt
- 1/2 tsp white pepper
- 1/2 tsp baking powder
- 4 cups of beef or chicken broth
- Noodles, vegetables, and fried shallots for serving

Instructions:
1. The ground meat, tapioca flour, egg, chop-up garlic, salt, white pepper, and baking powder Must all be combined in a combining dish. Combine thoroughly up to the Mixture starts to stick.
2. Form the Mixture into tiny meatballs with damp palms.
3. In a pot, bring the broth to a boil. The meatballs Must be added and cooked up to they float to the top. It ought Must take five to seven mins.
4. Divide your choice noodles among serving dishes after cooking them per the directions on the box/pkg.
5. Over the noodles, spoon the broth and meatballs.
6. Along with fried shallots and blanched vegetables, serve the bakso.

NUTRITION INFO: (Per Serving, approximate)
Cals: 300 kcal, Protein: 15g
Carbs: 20g, Fat: 18g, Fiber: 1g

65. Terang Bulan (Indonesian Pancake)

Prep Time: 15 mins
Cook Time: 15 mins
Total Time: 30 mins
Servings: 2-4 (depending on size)

Ingredients:
- 1 cup of all-purpose flour
- 1/2 cup of granulated sugar
- 1/2 tsp salt
- 1 tsp baking powder
- 2/3 cup of milk
- 1 egg
- 1 tsp vanilla extract
- Butter or oil, for cooking
- Toppings of your choice (chocolate, cheese, condensed milk, etc.)

Instructions:
1. Combine the flour, sugar, salt, and baking powder in a bowl.

2. Whisk the milk, egg, and vanilla essence in a separate basin.
3. Whisking constantly, gradually incorporate the wet components into the dry ones. Avoid overcombining; a few lumps are acceptable.
4. A nonstick pan Must be heated to medium. Put a little butter or oil in.
5. A ladleful of the batter Must be poured into the pan, and it Must be swirled to form an even, thin coating.
6. Cook for two to three mins, or up to surface bubbles appear and the edges begin to lift.
7. Add your preferred toppings to the pancake.
8. When the other side is golden brown, carefully flip the pancake over and cook for an additional 1-2 mins.
9. With the leftover batter and toppings, repeat the procedure.
10. Warm, folded or rolled terang bulan Must be served.

NUTRITION INFO: (Per Serving, approximate)
Cals: 250 kcal, Protein: 6g
Carbs: 45g, Fat: 5g, Fiber: 1g

66. Tahu Campur (Tofu and Bean Sprout Salad)

Prep Time: 15 mins
Cook Time: 10 mins
Total Time: 25 mins
Servings: 4

Ingredients:

- 300g firm tofu, slice into cubes
- 150g bean sprouts, cleaned
- 1 cucumber, julienned
- 2 boiled eggs, split
- 4 tbsp sweet soy sauce (kecap manis)
- 2 tbsp vegetable oil
- 2 cloves garlic, chop-up
- 1 red chili, split
- Salt and pepper as needed
- Fried shallots for garnish

Instructions:

1. Oil in a pan is heated to medium heat. Cook the tofu cubes till golden brown after adding them. Take out of the pan and place aside.
2. Split chile and chop-up garlic Must be cooked together in the same pan up to aromatic.
3. Add a dash of salt and the bean sprouts. Cook up to slightly wilted, about 1-2 mins.
4. On a serving platter, arrange the tofu, bean sprouts, julienned cucumber, and split boiled eggs.

5. Add sweet soy sauce to the dish's ingredients.
6. Add fried shallots as a garnish.
7. Tahu Campur Must be served quickly.

Nutrition (per serving):
Cals: 250 kcal, Protein: 12g
Carbs: 18g, Fat: 15g, Fiber: 3g

67. Sate Maranggi (Grilled Beef Skewers)

Prep Time: 20 mins
Cook Time: 15 mins
Total Time: 35 mins
Servings: 6

Ingredients:

- 500g beef sirloin, thinly split
- 3 shallots, lightly chop-up
- 3 cloves garlic, chop-up
- 2 tbsp sweet soy sauce (kecap manis)
- 1 tbsp soy sauce
- 1 tbsp tamarind paste
- 1 tsp ground coriander
- 1 tsp ground cumin
- 1 tsp turmeric powder
- 1 tsp brown sugar
- Bamboo skewers, soaked in water
- Salt and pepper as needed

Instructions:

1. Shallots that have been chop-up, garlic that has been chop-up, soy sauce, sweet soy sauce, tamarind paste, ground coriander, ground cumin, turmeric powder, brown sugar, salt, and pepper Must all be combined in a bowl. To make a marinade, thoroughly combine.
2. Add the meat, which has been thinly split, to the marinade, evenly coating every piece. In the refrigerator, let it marinade for at least an hr but preferably longer.
3. On the wet bamboo skewers, thread the beef slices that have been marinated.
4. A grill or grill pan Must be preheated to high heat.
5. For the steak to be cooked to the proper doneness, grill the skewers for 2 to 3 mins on every side.
6. Steamed rice and your preferred sambal Must be served with the sate maranggi.

Nutrition (per serving):
Cals: 220 kcal, Protein: 20g, Carbs: 8g, Fat: 12g
Fiber: 1g

68. Sop Kaki Kambing (Goat Feet Soup)

Prep Time: 30 mins

Cook Time 2 hrs

Total Time: 2 hrs 30 mins

Servings: 8

Ingredients:

- 1 kg goat feet, cleaned and chop-up
- 1 onion, chop-up
- 3 cloves garlic, chop-up
- 2 tomatoes, diced
- 2 carrots, peel off and split
- 2 potatoes, peel off and diced
- 2 lemongrass stalks, bruised
- 3 kaffir lime leaves
- 1-inch ginger, split
- 1 tsp ground coriander
- 1 tsp ground cumin
- Salt and pepper as needed
- Water
- Fried shallots for garnish
- Chop-up fresh cilantro for garnish

Instructions:

1. Boiling water Must be used in a big pot to blanch the chop-up goat feet for a few mins. Drain, then set apart.
2. Heat some oil in the same pan and cook the chop-up garlic and onion up to fragrant.
3. For a few mins, add the goat feet that have been blanched.
4. The goat's feet Must be covered with water. After bringing to a boil, turn down the heat to a simmer.
5. Add the chop-up ginger, ground coriander, ground cumin, salt, and pepper, along with the chop-up tomatoes, split carrots, diced potatoes, and lemongrass stalks.
6. Once the flavors are blended and the goat feet are soft, let the soup simmer for about two hrs.
7. Any contaminants that appear during cooking Must be skimmed off.
8. Serve the Sop Kaki Kambing hot, topped with chop-up cilantro and fried shallots.

Nutrition (per serving):

Cals: 300 kcal, Protein: 18g, Carbs: 15g

Fat: 20g, Fiber: 3g

69. Sambal Goreng Kentang Ati (Potato and Liver in Spicy Sauce)

Prep Time: 15 mins

Cook Time: 30 mins

Total Time: 45 mins

Servings: 4

Ingredients:

- 2 medium potatoes, peel off and diced
- 200g chicken or beef liver, cleaned and split
- 3 shallots, thinly split
- 3 cloves garlic, chop-up
- 2 red chili peppers, split
- 2 green chili peppers, split
- 2 kaffir lime leaves, lightly chop-up
- 1 lemongrass stalk, bruised
- 1 tsp shrimp paste (non-compulsory)
- 1 tsp tamarind paste
- 1 tsp sugar
- Salt as needed
- Cooking oil

Instructions:

1. The potatoes Must be chop-up and fried in hot oil up to golden brown. Take out and place aside.
2. Cook the liver slices in the same skillet. Take out and place aside.
3. The shallots, garlic, and red and green chili peppers Must be sautéed in some oil in a separate pan up to aromatic.
4. Add the salt, sugar, tamarind paste, shrimp paste, kaffir lime leaves, and lemongrass. Combine thoroughly.
5. Add the liver and fried potatoes to the pan. Stir-fry for a few mins to thoroughly combine and warm up the ingredients.
6. With hot rice, serve.

Nutrition (per serving):

Cals: ~250 kcal, Protein: ~12g

Fat: ~10g, Carbs: ~30g, Fiber: ~4g

70. Tahu Telur Betawi (Betawi-style Tofu Omelette)

Prep Time: 15 mins

Cook Time: 20 mins

Total Time: 35 mins

Servings: 6

Ingredients:

- 300g firm tofu, diced
- 4 eggs
- 2 shallots, thinly split
- 3 cloves garlic, chop-up
- 2 green onions, chop-up
- 1 mini carrot, finely grated
- 1 tsp salt
- 1/2 tsp white pepper
- Cooking oil

Instructions:

1. Whisk the eggs in a bowl before adding the tofu dice. Combine slowly.
2. The tofu and egg combination is added to a pan that has been heated with oil. Cook up to the bottom is golden brown on medium heat.
3. The omelette Must be flipped over and cooked up to golden brown on both sides.
4. The shallots and garlic Must be sautéed up to aromatic in another pan.
5. After adding, boil the finely grated carrot for a short while.
6. After seasoning with salt and pepper, add the cooked vegetables on top of the omelette.
7. Add chop-up green onions as a garnish.
8. Slice, then dish.

Nutrition (per serving):
Cals: ~180 kcal, Protein: ~12g

Fat: ~12g, Carbs: ~7g, Fiber: ~2g

71. Bika Ambon (Indonesian Honeycomb Cake)

Prep Time: 15 mins

Cook Time: 1 hr

Total Time: 1 hr 15 mins

Servings: 8

Ingredients:

- 250g tapioca flour
- 150g all-purpose flour
- 200g granulated sugar
- 400ml coconut milk
- 4 eggs
- 1 tsp yeast
- 1/2 tsp vanilla extract
- 1/4 tsp salt
- Pandan leaves for aroma (non-compulsory)
- Yellow food coloring (non-compulsory)
- Margarine or butter for greasing

Instructions:

1. Combine yeast, all-purpose flour, and tapioca flour in a bowl.
2. Coconut milk and sugar are heated in a pot over low heat up to the sugar is dissolved. Take it off the fire and give it a min to cool.
3. To prevent lumps, continuously stir the flour Mixture while you gradually add the coconut milk Mixture.
4. After every addition, thoroughly combine in the eggs one at a time.
5. Salt, pandan leaves, and vanilla extract can all be added.

6. To get the classic color, you could optionally add a few drops of yellow food coloring.
7. To make sure the batter is lump-free and smooth, strain it.
8. Give the batter about an hr to rest.
9. Set the oven's temperature to 180 C (350 F).
10. A circular cake pan Must be greased with butter or margarine.
11. The cake Must be cooked and the top Must be golden brown, so pour the batter into the pan and bake it in the preheated oven for 45 to 60 mins.
12. Before slicing and serving, let the cake cool.

Nutrition (per serving):
Cals: ~300 kcal, Protein: ~4g

Fat: ~10g, Carbs: ~50g, Fiber: ~1g

72. Coto Makassar (Makassar Beef Soup)

Prep Time: 20 mins

Cook Time: 2 hrs

Total Time: 2 hrs 20 mins

Servings: 6

Ingredients:

- 500g beef, slice into chunks
- 200g beef tripe, cleaned and boiled (non-compulsory)
- 100g rice noodles, cooked according to box/pkg instructions
- 4 shallots, chop-up
- 3 cloves garlic, chop-up
- 2 lemongrass stalks, bruised
- 2 cm galangal, split
- 3 kaffir lime leaves
- 1 tsp ground turmeric
- 1 tsp ground coriander
- 1/2 tsp ground cumin
- 1/2 tsp ground cinnamon
- 1/4 tsp ground cloves
- 1/4 tsp ground nutmeg
- Salt as needed
- Cooking oil
- Fried shallots and celery leaves for garnish

Instructions:

1. Heat some oil in a pot, then cook the chop-up shallots and garlic up to they are aromatic.
2. Brown the meat chunks all over after adding them.
3. Spices, galangal, kaffir lime leaves, and lemongrass Must be added. For a few mins, stir-fry.
4. Bring to a boil the beef with just enough water to cover it.

5. Once the beef is cooked, lower the heat and let the soup simmer for 1.5 to 2 hrs. Tripe Must be added in the final hr of cooking if using.
6. Depending on your taste, salt the soup.
7. Place some cooked rice noodles in a bowl, then top with beef and liquid to serve.
8. Add celery leaves and fried shallots as a garnish.

Nutrition (per serving):

Cals: ~400 kcal, Protein: ~20g

Fat: ~15g, Carbs: ~45g, Fiber: ~3g

73.Es Teler (Indonesian Fruit Cocktail)

Prep Time: 15 mins

Cook Time: 0 mins

Total Time: 15 mins

Servings: 4

Ingredients:

- 1 ripe avocado, diced
- 1 ripe jackfruit, diced
- 1 cup of young coconut meat, thinly split
- 1 cup of sweetened condensed milk
- 1 cup of coconut milk
- 1/2 cup of diced cantaloupe
- 1/2 cup of diced pineapple
- 1/2 cup of diced honeydew melon
- 1/2 cup of ice cubes
- 1/4 cup of sugar (adjust as needed)
- 1/4 tsp salt

Instructions:

1. The diced avocado, jackfruit, young coconut meat, cantaloupe, pineapple, and honeydew melon Must all be combined in a sizable combining dish.
2. The sweetened condensed milk, coconut milk, sugar, and salt Must all be thoroughly blended in a different bowl. As needed, adjust the sugar.
3. Fruits Must be lightly coated with the milk Mixture by pouring it over them and tossing them.
4. Gently whisk in the ice cubes after adding the Mixture.
5. In individual serving glasses or bowls, present the Es Teler.

74.Rujak Manis (Sweet Fruit Salad)

Prep Time: 20 mins

Cook Time: 0 mins

Total Time: 20 mins

Servings: 4

Ingredients:

- 2 apples, julienned
- 2 pears, julienned
- 2 oranges, segmented
- 1 cucumber, julienned
- 1 cup of pineapple chunks
- 1 cup of jicama, julienned
- 1 cup of mango chunks
- 1 cup of roasted peanuts, crushed
- 1 cup of palm sugar, finely grated
- 1 tsp shrimp paste (non-compulsory)
- 3-4 red chili peppers, split
- Salt as needed

Instructions:

1. The julienned apples, pears, cucumber, and jicama Must all be combined in a big bowl.
2. Orange segments, pineapple pieces, and mango chunks Must all be added to the bowl.
3. To make a dressing, combine the shredded palm sugar, split chile peppers, shrimp paste (if using), and a dash of salt in a different bowl.
4. The fruit Mixture Must be covered well after the dressing has been added.
5. Just before serving, top the salad with the crushed roasted peanuts.
6. Serve the fruit salad right away.

NUTRITION INFO (per serving):

Cals: 220, Carbs: 40g

Protein: 4g, Fat: 7g, Fiber: 6g

75. Pindang Patin (Spiced Catfish Stew)

Prep Time: 15 mins

Cook Time: 40 mins

Total Time: 55 mins

Servings: 4

Ingredients:

- 4 catfish fillets
- 2 tomatoes, chop-up
- 1 lemongrass stalk, bruised
- 4 kaffir lime leaves
- 2 tbsp tamarind paste
- 1 tsp palm sugar
- 4 cups of water
- Salt as needed
- Spice Paste:
- 4 shallots
- 3 cloves garlic
- 2 red chili peppers
- 1 inch ginger
- 1 inch turmeric

Instructions:

1. In a mixer, combine the spice paste components up to they are well-combined.
2. The spice paste, water, diced tomatoes, lemongrass, kaffir lime leaves, tamarind paste, and palm sugar Must all be combined in a pot. Simmer for a while.
3. Cook the catfish fillets in the pot for 20 to 25 mins, or up to they are cooked through and are soft.
4. As needed, add salt to the dish.
5. Warm steamed rice Must be served with the spicy catfish stew.

NUTRITION INFO (per serving):
Cals: 290, Carbs: 14g

Protein: 30g, Fat: 12g, Fiber: 2g

76. Asinan (Pickled Vegetable Salad)

Prep Time: 30 mins

Cook Time: 10 mins

Total Time: 40 mins

Servings: 6

Ingredients:

- 2 cups of cabbage, thinly split
- 1 cup of carrots, julienned
- 1 cup of cucumber, julienned
- 1 cup of bean sprouts
- 1 cup of pineapple, chop-up
- 1 cup of fried tofu, cubed
- 1/2 cup of roasted peanuts, crushed
- 3 bird's eye chili peppers, chop-up (adjust as needed)
- Pickling Solution:
- 1 cup of water
- 1 cup of vinegar
- 1/2 cup of palm sugar
- 1/2 tsp salt

Instructions:

1. Water, vinegar, palm sugar, and salt Must be combined in a pot. Bring to a boil while stirring to completely dissolve the sugar and salt. Let the pickling liquid to cool.
2. Split cabbage, carrots, cucumber, bean sprouts, pineapple, and fried tofu Must all be combined in a big bowl.
3. After the pickling solution has cooled, pour it over the veggies and toss to incorporate. Let it to marinade for 15 to 20 mins.
4. Serve the pickled vegetable salad in individual bowls with chop-up jalapeño peppers and cut up toasted peanuts as garnishes.

NUTRITION INFO (per serving):
Cals: 180, Carbs: 25g

Protein: 7g, Fat: 6g, Fiber: 4g

77. Rendang Sapi (Beef Rendang)

Prep Time: 20 mins

Cook Time: 3 hrs

Total Time: 3 hrs 20 mins

Servings: 6

Ingredients:

- 2 lbs beef chuck, slice into chunks
- 2 cans (14 oz every) coconut milk
- 4 kaffir lime leaves
- 2 lemongrass stalks, bruised
- 2 turmeric leaves (non-compulsory)
- 1 tamarind pulp, dissolved in 1/4 cup of water
- 2 tbsp oil
- Salt as needed
- Spice Paste:
- 6 shallots
- 4 cloves garlic
- 3 red chili peppers
- 3 dried chili peppers, soaked and deseeded
- 1 inch ginger
- 1 inch galangal
- 1 tsp ground coriander
- 1/2 tsp ground cumin
- 1/2 tsp ground turmeric

Instructions:

1. In a mixer, combine the spice paste components up to they are well-combined.
2. Heat the oil in a big pot, then sauté the spice paste up to it is aromatic.
3. When the beef chunks are added, sauté them up to both sides are browned.
4. Add the coconut milk, tamarind liquid, kaffir lime leaves, lemongrass, and (if using) turmeric leaves.
5. After bringing to a boil, turn down the heat. Cook the beef Mixture for 2.5 to 3 hrs, stirring regularly, up to the meat is cooked and the liquid has thickened.
6. Add salt as needed and cook for an additional 15 to 20 mins to achieve a rich, black sauce.
7. Take out the turmeric, lemongrass, and kaffir lime leaves.
8. Serve steaming rice alongside the beef rendang.

NUTRITION INFO (per serving):
Cals: 450, Carbs: 10g

Protein: 30g, Fat: 35g, Fiber: 2g

78. Perkedel Jagung (Corn Fritters)

Prep Time: 15 mins

Cook Time: 20 mins

Total Time: 35 mins

Servings: 4

Ingredients:

- 2 cups of fresh corn kernels
- 1/2 cup of all-purpose flour
- 2 shallots, lightly chop-up
- 2 cloves garlic, chop-up
- 1 tsp baking powder
- 1/2 tsp salt
- 1/4 tsp black pepper
- 1 egg, beaten
- Oil for frying

Instructions:

1. Corn kernels, chop-up garlic, chop-up shallots, all-purpose flour, baking soda, salt, and black pepper Must all be combined in a combining bowl.
2. Then, add the beaten egg and toss everything together thoroughly.
3. In a frying pan, heat the oil over medium-low heat.
4. Carefully drop spoonfuls of the corn Mixture into the hot oil.
5. The fritters Must be crispy and golden brown on both sides.
6. The fritters Must be taken out of the oil and placed on a dish covered with paper towels to absorb any extra oil.
7. While the corn fritters are still warm, serve them. You can serve them with your preferred dipping sauce or chili sauce.

Nutrition (per serving):

Cals: 180, Carbs: 28g

Protein: 5g, Fat: 6g, Fiber: 3g

79. Sate Rembiga (Lombok-style Satay)

Prep Time: 30 mins (+ marinating time)

Cook Time: 15 mins

Total Time: 45 mins (+ marinating time)

Servings: 6

Ingredients:

- 1 lb chicken or beef, slice into mini cubes
- 2 tbsp sweet soy sauce (kecap manis)
- 2 tbsp vegetable oil
- 1 tsp ground turmeric
- 1 tsp ground coriander
- 1/2 tsp ground cumin
- 1/2 tsp ground pepper
- 3 shallots, chop-up
- 2 cloves garlic, chop-up
- Bamboo skewers, soaked in water

Instructions:

1. To make the marinade, combine sweet soy sauce, vegetable oil, ground coriander, ground cumin, ground pepper, ground turmeric, ground coriander, ground cumin, ground pepper, chop-up garlic, and shallots.
2. Make sure the beef or chicken cubes are thoroughly coated before adding them to the marinade. Marinate for at least two hrs or refrigerate overnight.
3. The soaking bamboo skewers are then threaded with the marinated meat.
4. Over medium-high heat, grill or barbeque the skewers, rotating them regularly, for 10-15 mins, or up to the meat is cooked through and slightly browned.
5. With rice and a serving of sambal or peanut sauce, serve the sate rembiga hot.

Nutrition (per serving, chicken version):

Cals: 220, Carbs: 7g

Protein: 25g, Fat: 10g, Fiber: 1g

80. Soto Banjar (Banjarese Chicken Soup)

Prep Time: 20 mins

Cook Time: 1 hr

Total Time: 1 hr 20 mins

Servings: 4

Ingredients:

- 1 whole chicken, slice into pieces
- 8 cups of water
- 2 stalks lemongrass, bruised
- 3 kaffir lime leaves
- 3 cloves garlic, chop-up
- 1 onion, chop-up
- 1 tsp ground turmeric
- 1 tsp ground coriander
- Salt and pepper as needed
- Rice vermicelli, cooked according to box/pkg instructions
- Toppings: fried shallots, chop-up scallions, chop-up cilantro, lime wedges

Instructions:

1. Chicken chunks, water, lemongrass, kaffir lime leaves, chop-up garlic, onion, turmeric, and ground coriander are all combined in a saucepan.
2. When the chicken is cooked and the flavors are blended, bring the Mixture to a boil, then lower the heat and let it simmer for 45 to 60 mins.
3. Shred the chicken after removing the chunks from the soup. Return the shredded chicken to the broth and discard the bones.

4. Add salt and pepper as needed when preparing the soup.
5. Pour the hot soup over the cooked rice vermicelli in bowls, garnish with fried shallots, chop-up scallions, chop-up cilantro, and a squeeze of lime, and serve immediately.

Nutrition (per serving):
Cals: 300, Carbs: 25g
Protein: 30g, Fat: 10g, Fiber: 2g

81. Klepon Ketan Hitam (Black Glutinous Rice Cake with Palm Sugar)

Prep Time: 1 hr
Cook Time: 30 mins
Total Time: 1 hr 30 mins
Servings: 12

Ingredients:
- 2 cups of black glutinous rice, soaked overnight
- 1 cup of palm sugar, chop-up
- 1/2 cup of finely grated coconut, steamed and combined with a pinch of salt
- Banana leaves, slice into mini squares and briefly passed over an open flame to soften

Instructions:
1. Once the glutinous rice has been soaked, drain it and steam it for 20 to 25 mins, or up to it is cooked and soft.
2. Lb or mash the rice while it's still heated to create a smooth dough-like texture.
3. In your palm, flatten a tiny amount of the rice dough.
4. Wrap the rice dough around a piece of lightly chop-up palm sugar in the center to create a little ball.
5. Apply the same procedure to the remaining palm sugar and rice dough.
6. Gently coat the rice balls with the finely grated coconut by gently rolling them in it.
7. To preserve its shape, every rice ball Must be wrapped in a piece of banana leaf.
8. The Klepon Ketan Hitam Must be served at room temperature.

Nutrition (per serving):
Cals: 180, Carbs: 40g, Protein: 2g, Fat: 2g
Fiber: 2g

82. Tumis Bunga Pepaya (Stir-fried Papaya Flowers)

Prep Time: 20 mins
Cook Time: 15 mins
Total Time: 35 mins
Servings: 4

Ingredients:
- 2 cups of papaya flowers, cleaned and chop-up
- 1 mini onion, thinly split
- 2 cloves garlic, chop-up
- 2 red chili peppers, split
- 1 tbsp shrimp paste (terasi), toasted
- 2 tbsp cooking oil
- Salt as needed

Instructions:
1. The roasted shrimp paste Must be well ground in a pestle and mortar. Place aside.
2. Over medium heat, warm the cooking oil in the pan. Add the onion slices and garlic powder. Sauté up to the onion is transparent and aromatic.
3. Split chile peppers and ground shrimp paste Must be added. Stir-fry for a min to ensure complete blending.
4. To the pan, add the chop-up papaya flowers. Stir-fry the flowers for 5 to 7 mins, or up to they are soft.
5. As needed, add salt to the dish. After one last stir, turn off the heat.
6. Rice Must be served with the Tumis Bunga Pepaya as a side dish.

83. Lontong Sayur (Rice Cake in Coconut Broth)

Prep Time: 30 mins
Cook Time: 1 hr
Total Time: 1 hr 30 mins
Servings: 6

Ingredients:
- 2 cups of rice, soaked and drained
- Banana leaves or plastic wrap
- 400 ml coconut milk
- 4 cups of vegetable broth
- 200g tofu, cubed
- 150g tempeh, split
- 200g bean sprouts
- 2 cups of combined vegetables (cabbage, carrots, long beans), split
- 3 shallots, thinly split
- 2 cloves garlic, chop-up
- 1 tsp turmeric powder
- 2 bay leaves
- Salt and sugar as needed
- Fried shallots and prawn crackers for garnish

1. Rice that has been soaked Must be placed into the cylinders made from banana leaves or plastic wrap. Kitchen twine Must be used to tie off the ends.
2. The rice cylinders Must be cooked after roughly an hr of boiling. Slice them into bite-sized pieces after they have cooled.
3. Split shallots and chop-up garlic Must be sautéed in a pot up to aromatic. Stir in the bay leaves, coconut milk, and vegetable broth after adding the turmeric powder.
4. Add combined vegetables, tofu, and tempeh to the saucepan. Simmer it for a while to cook the vegetables.
5. Add cooked rice cake slices and bean sprouts. As needed, add salt and sugar to the dish.
6. Serve the Lontong Sayur hot with prawn crackers and shallots that have been cooked.

84. Sambal Terasi (Shrimp Paste Chili Sauce)

Prep Time: 15 mins
Cook Time: 10 mins
Total Time: 25 mins
Servings: 8

Ingredients:

- 10 red chili peppers, seeded and chop-up
- 5 bird's eye chili peppers (adjust as needed)
- 3 cloves garlic
- 1 tsp shrimp paste (terasi), toasted
- 1 mini tomato, chop-up
- 1 tsp sugar
- Juice of 1 lime
- Salt as needed

Instructions:

1. Grind the red chili peppers, bird's eye chili peppers, garlic, and toasted shrimp paste into a paste using a mortar and pestle.
2. When you've thoroughly blended it, add the diced tomato to the paste and keep grinding.
3. Incorporate the paste into a bowl. Include salt, lime juice, and sugar. Completely combine.
4. To suit your personal preferences, adjust the seasoning.
5. Serve the Sambal Terasi with various Indonesian cuisines as a condiment.

Nutrition (per serving):
Cals: 15 kcal, Carbs: 3g
Protein: 1gFat: 0g, Fiber: 1g

85. Pepes Jamur (Steamed Mushroom in Banana Leaves)

Prep Time: 30 mins
Cook Time: 20 mins
Total Time: 50 mins
Servings: 4

Ingredients:

- 400g mushrooms (shiitake, oyster, or your choice), cleaned and split
- 2 shallots, thinly split
- 2 cloves garlic, chop-up
- 2 red chili peppers, split
- 2 kaffir lime leaves, thinly split
- 1 lemongrass stalk, white part only, bruised
- 1 tsp turmeric powder
- Salt and sugar as needed
- Banana leaves or aluminum foil, slice into squares

Instructions:

1. Split mushrooms, shallots, garlic, red chile peppers, kaffir lime leaves, and lemongrass Must all be combined in a bowl.
2. Salt, sugar, and turmeric powder Must be added to the Mixture. Combine vigorously to evenly distribute the spices over the mushrooms.
3. A portion of the mushroom Mixture Must be placed in the center of a piece of aluminum foil or a banana leaf. In order to produce a sealed packet, fold and fasten the edges.
4. For the remaining mushroom combination, repeat the procedure.
5. For around 15 to 20 mins, cook the banana leaf box/pkgs in a steamer up to the mushrooms are flavorful and soft.
6. Open the box/pkgs with caution, then move the Pepes Jamur to a serving platter.
7. The Pepes Jamur is delicious as a starter or side dish.

Nutrition (per serving):
Cals: 50 kcal, Carbs: 12g
Protein: 2g, Fat: 0g, Fiber: 2g

86.Gulai Ayam (Chicken Curry)

Prep Time: 20 mins
Cook Time: 1 hr
Total Time: 1 hr 20 mins
Servings: 4

Ingredients:

- 1 kg chicken pieces, cleaned and slice
- 2 cups of coconut milk
- 2 tbsp oil
- 2 onions, lightly chop-up

- 3 cloves garlic, chop-up
- 1 tsp ginger paste
- 2 tsp ground coriander
- 1 tsp ground turmeric
- 1 tsp chili powder
- 1 tsp cumin powder
- 2 lemongrass stalks, bruised
- 4 kaffir lime leaves
- Salt as needed
- Sugar as needed
- 1 cup of water

Instructions:

1. The chop-up onions, chop-up garlic, and ginger paste Must be sautéed in hot oil up to aromatic.
2. Cook the chicken chunks after adding them up to they begin to brown.
3. Stir in the ground coriander, turmeric, cumin, and chili powder. Combine thoroughly to distribute the seasonings throughout the chicken.
4. Add the water and coconut milk. Add lemongrass stalks and kaffir lime leaves after stirring.
5. As needed, add salt and sugar to the dish. Once the chicken is cooked and the flavors are blended, give the curry an hr or so to simmer on medium heat.
6. With steamed rice, serve the chicken curry.

NUTRITION INFO:

Cals: 350 per serving, Protein: 25g

Carbs: 10g, Fat: 25g

87. Bubur Candil (Sweet Rice Balls in Palm Sugar Syrup)

Prep Time: 30 mins

Cook Time: 30 mins

Total Time: 1 hr

Servings: 4

Ingredients:

- 1 cup of glutinous rice flour
- 1/4 cup of tapioca flour
- 1/2 cup of water
- 1/2 cup of finely grated coconut
- 1/2 cup of palm sugar, chop-up
- A pinch of salt
- Pandan leaves (non-compulsory), for aroma

Instructions:

1. Combine tapioca flour and glutinous rice flour in a combining dish.
2. Add water gradually while combining the ingredients to form a homogeneous dough.
3. Make little balls out of the dough by taking little amounts. Place aside.

4. Cook the rice balls in a pot of boiling water up to they float to the top. Take out and place aside.
5. Bring water, palm sugar, and a dash of salt to a boil in a separate pot. The palm sugar must be thoroughly dissolved by stirring.
6. As the syrup simmers for a few mins to slightly thicken, add pandan leaves for flavor.
7. Put the cooked rice balls in serving bowls, cover them with palm sugar syrup, and top with finely grated coconut to serve.
8. While they're still warm, savor the delicious rice balls in palm sugar syrup.

Nutrition (per serving):

Cals: 250 kcal, Carbs: 57 g

Fat: 3 g, Protein: 2 g, Fiber: 1 g

88. Tahu Bacem (Sweet Soy Glazed Tofu)

Prep Time: 15 mins

Cook Time: 20 mins

Total Time: 35 mins

Servings: 3-4

Ingredients:

- 1 block firm tofu, slice into rectangles
- 3 tbsp sweet soy sauce (kecap manis)
- 1 tbsp tamarind paste
- 2 cloves garlic, chop-up
- 1/2 tsp coriander powder
- 1/2 tsp salt
- 1/4 tsp pepper
- 1 cup of water
- Cooking oil

Instructions:

1. To prepare the marinade, combine the sweet soy sauce, tamarind paste, chop-up garlic, coriander powder, salt, and pepper in a bowl.
2. For about 10 mins, let the tofu rectangles soak up the Mixture.
3. Cooking oil Must be hot before adding the marinated tofu to the pan to fry. Take out of the pan and place aside.
4. Add water and the remaining marinade to the same pan. up to a boil.
5. Return the fried tofu to the pan after it has boiled. Simmer the sauce for a while over low heat, coating the tofu as it gets thicker.
6. Tofu Must be coated uniformly with the sauce by stirring from time to time to avoid sticking.
7. Take out from heat once the sauce has thickened and the tofu is coated.
8. Serve steamed rice beside the Tahu Bacem.

Nutrition (per serving):

Cals: 180 kcal, Carbs: 20 g, Fat: 10 g

Protein: 7 g, Fiber: 1 g

89. Nasi Jagung (Corn Rice)

Prep Time: 10 mins

Cook Time: 20 mins

Total Time: 30 mins

Servings: 4

Ingredients:

- 2 cups of cooked white rice
- 1 cup of corn kernels (fresh, refrigerate, or canned)
- 1 mini onion, lightly chop-up
- 2 cloves garlic, chop-up
- 2 tbsp cooking oil
- Salt as needed
- Chop-up cilantro for garnish

Instructions:

1. Cooking oil Must be heated in a pan over medium heat.
2. Add the chop-up garlic and onion, both chop-up. till translucent and aromatic, sauté.
3. The corn kernels Must be heated through after being added and cooked for a few mins.
4. Combine the corn, onion, and garlic Mixture well with the cooked white rice before adding it to the pan.
5. Add salt as needed and simmer for a short while longer, stirring occasionally.
6. Take out from heat once everything has been heated and combined properly.
7. Before serving, garnish with chop-up cilantro.
8. Nasi Jagung, a savory side dish, is prepared to be served.

Nutrition (per serving):

Cals: 220 kcal, Carbs: 38 g, Fat 6 g, Protein: 4 g, Fiber: 2 g

90. Karedok Bantal (Raw Vegetable Salad with Peanut Sauce)

Prep Time: 20 mins

Cook Time: 0 mins

Total Time: 20 mins

Servings: 4

Ingredients:

For the Salad:

- 2 cups of bean sprouts
- 1 cup of cucumber, julienned
- 1 cup of cabbage, thinly split
- 1 cup of long beans, slice into 2-inch pieces
- 1 cup of tofu, boiled and slice into cubes
- 1 cup of tempeh, boiled and slice into cubes
- 1 cup of Thai basil leaves

For the Peanut Sauce:

- 1 cup of roasted peanuts
- 2 cloves garlic
- 2-3 red chillies (adjust as needed)
- 1 tsp tamarind paste
- 1 tsp palm sugar or brown sugar
- Salt as needed
- Water

Instructions:

1. On a serving tray, prepare all the vegetables and arrange them accordingly.
2. Roasted peanuts, garlic, red peppers, tamarind paste, palm sugar, and a dash of salt Must all be combined in a blender or mixer.
3. To create a smooth and thick peanut sauce, blend the ingredients while gradually adding water.
4. Taste the peanut sauce and make any necessary flavor adjustments.
5. Over the prepared vegetables, drizzle the peanut sauce.
6. You can eat the Karedok Bantal alone or with rice.

Nutrition (per serving):

Cals: 300 kcal, Carbs: 20 g

Fat: 22 g, Protein: 14 g, Fiber: 5 g

91. Rujak Juhi (Squid Salad with Peanut Sauce)

Prep Time: 20 mins

Cook Time: 10 mins

Total Time: 30 mins

Servings: 4

Ingredients:

- 300g squid, cleaned and split into rings
- 1 cup of cucumber, julienned
- 1 cup of pineapple, diced
- 1 cup of jicama (yam bean), julienned
- 1 cup of bean sprouts
- 1/2 cup of roasted peanuts, crushed
- 2 red chillies, split
- 1/4 cup of tamarind pulp
- 2 tbsp palm sugar
- Salt as needed
- Peanut Sauce:
- 1 cup of roasted peanuts, ground
- 3 cloves garlic
- 2 red chillies
- 2 tbsp palm sugar
- 1 tsp shrimp paste
- Salt as needed

Instructions:

1. To make tamarind juice, combine tamarind pulp and water. Discard seeds after straining.
2. Over low heat, combine palm sugar and tamarind juice in a mini pot. As needed, add salt. The sauce will thicken as it simmers. Place aside.
3. Blend the roasted peanuts, garlic, red pepper flakes, palm sugar, and shrimp paste together to make the peanut sauce. If necessary, add water to get the desired consistency. As needed, add salt.
4. Squid rings Must be cooked after around 1-2 mins of blanching in a kettle of boiling water. Drain, then set apart.
5. Blanched squid, cucumber, pineapple, jicama, bean sprouts, and thinly split red chilies Must all be combined in a big combining basin.
6. Sprinkle smashed toasted peanuts on top and toss the salad with the peanut sauce.
7. The tamarind sauce Must be served alongside the squid salad.

NUTRITION INFO:

Cals: 250, Protein: 15g

Carbs: 25g

Fat: 12g, Fiber: 5g

92. Rendang Kambing (Lamb Rendang)

Prep Time: 20 mins

Cook Time: 3 hrs

Total Time: 3 hrs 20 mins

Servings: 6

Ingredients:

- 1 kg lamb, slice into chunks
- 2 cans coconut milk (800ml)
- 3 kaffir lime leaves
- 2 lemongrass stalks, bruised
- 1 turmeric leaf (non-compulsory), torn
- Salt as needed
- Spice Paste:
- 6 shallots
- 4 cloves garlic
- 2 red chillies
- 3 dried chillies, soaked and deseeded
- 1 thumb-sized ginger
- 1 thumb-sized galangal
- 1 thumb-sized turmeric
- 1 tsp coriander powder
- 1/2 tsp cumin powder
- 1/2 tsp fennel powder
- 3 cloves
- 3 cardamom pods
- 1 cinnamon stick

Instructions:

1. Make a smooth Mixture out of all the ingredients for the spice paste.
2. The spice paste Must be sautéed in hot oil up to aromatic.
3. Cook the lamb chunks up to they change color after being added.
4. Lemongrass, turmeric leaf, and kaffir lime leaves are added after pouring in the coconut milk. Stir thoroughly.
5. Bring to a boil, lower the heat to a simmer, and cook for two to three hrs, or up to the beef is fork-tender and the sauce is thick. To avoid sticking, stir every so while.
6. Continue cooking while stirring often after the sauce has reduced and the meat is cooked up to the sauce is black, thick, and coating the meat.
7. As needed, add salt to the dish. If preferred, take out the whole spices.
8. Serve steaming rice alongside the beef rendang.

NUTRITION INFO:

Cals: 400, Protein: 20g

Carbs: 10g

Fat: 30g, Fiber: 2g

93. Nasi Urap (Combined Vegetable Rice)

Prep Time: 30 mins

Cook Time: 30 mins

Total Time: 1 hr

Servings: 4

Ingredients:

- 2 cups of cooked rice, cooled
- 1 cup of bean sprouts, blanched
- 1 cup of spinach, blanched and chop-up
- 1 cup of finely grated coconut, toasted
- 2 kaffir lime leaves, lightly split
- 2 tbsp fried shallots
- Salt as needed
- Spice Paste:
- 3 shallots
- 2 cloves garlic
- 2 red chillies
- 1 tsp shrimp paste
- 1 tsp palm sugar

Instructions:

1. Make a smooth Mixture out of all the ingredients for the spice paste.
2. The spice paste Must be sautéed in a hot skillet up to aromatic.
3. The pan Must now contain the bean sprouts and blanched spinach. To evenly distribute the spice paste, stir the vegetables well.

4. Add the toasted finely grated coconut and the cooked rice. Completely combine.
5. Add salt as needed and combine well.
6. Take out from fire and top with more toasted coconut, fried shallots, and kaffir lime leaves.
7. Your choice of protein or side dishes Must go with the rice with combined vegetables.

NUTRITION INFO:
Cals: 300, Protein: 6g
Carbs: 40g
Fat: 14g, Fiber: 3g

94. Tahu Isi (Stuffed Tofu)

Prep Time: 20 mins

Cook Time: 20 mins

Total Time: 40 mins

Servings: 4

Ingredients:

- 8 tofu blocks, firm or extra-firm
- 100g ground chicken or pork
- 1 carrot, lightly diced
- 1 onion, lightly diced
- 2 cloves garlic, chop-up
- 2 tbsp cooking oil
- 1 tsp soy sauce
- 1 tsp oyster sauce
- Salt and pepper as needed
- Batter:
- 1/2 cup of all-purpose flour
- 1/4 cup of water
- A pinch of salt

Instructions:

1. Every block of tofu Must have a pocket slice out for filling.
2. Garlic is sautéed in hot oil up to aromatic. When the onions are transparent, add them.
3. Cook up to browned after adding the ground meat.
4. Salt, pepper, soy sauce, oyster sauce, and carrots Must be added. Cook the carrots up to they are soft. Take it off the stove and let it cool.
5. Put the cooked filling inside the tofu pockets.
6. Up to the batter is smooth, combine the ingredients in a bowl.
7. In a pan, heat the oil. Every stuffed tofu piece Must be battered before being fried up to crispy and golden brown
8. Take out and drain on paper towels after leaving the oil.
9. Serve the filled tofu as an appetizer or as a snack.

NUTRITION INFO:
Cals: 220, Protein: 10g
Carbs: 15g
Fat: 14g, Fiber: 2g

95.Sate Plecing (Lombok-style Spicy Satay)

Prep Time: 20 mins

Cook Time: 15 mins

Total Time: 35 mins

Servings: 4

Ingredients:

- 500g chicken or beef, slice into mini cubes
- 20 bamboo skewers, soaked in water
- 3 shallots, chop-up
- 3 cloves garlic, chop-up
- 2 red chillies, chop-up
- 2 tomatoes, chop-up
- 2 tsp shrimp paste (terasi)
- 1 tsp palm sugar or brown sugar
- 1 tsp salt
- 1 tsp pepper
- 2 tbsp vegetable oil
- Lime wedges, for serving

Instructions:

1. To make a marinade, combine the chop-up shallots, garlic, red pepper flakes, shrimp paste, salt, and pepper in a basin.
2. To the moistened bamboo skewers, thread the meat.
3. After applying the marinade, give the meat a good 15 mins to settle.
4. On a barbecue or on a grill pan, heat the vegetable oil.
5. The skewers Must be cooked through and slightly browned after grilling for 10 to 15 mins, rotating them once.
6. To prepare the plecing sauce, combine chop-up tomatoes, palm sugar, and a dash of salt in a different bowl.
7. Serve wedges of lime and plecing sauce alongside the grilled satay.

Nutrition (per serving): (approximate values)
Cals: 250, Protein: 20g, Fat: 12g
Carbs: 15g, Fiber: 2g

96. Soto Sulung (Sulung Beef Soup)

Prep Time: 30 mins

Cook Time: 2 hrs

Total Time: 2 hrs 30 mins

Servings: 6

Ingredients:

- 500g beef shank or stewing beef, slice into chunks
- 2 lemongrass stalks, bruised
- 3 kaffir lime leaves
- 3 cloves garlic, chop-up
- 2 shallots, chop-up
- 1 tsp ground turmeric
- 1 tsp ground coriander
- 1/2 tsp ground cumin
- 4 cups of beef broth
- 2 potatoes, peel off and slice into chunks
- 2 carrots, peel off and split
- 100g bean sprouts
- 2 hard-boiled eggs, halved
- Fried shallots, for garnish
- Fresh cilantro, chop-up, for garnish
- Salt and pepper as needed
- Cooking oil

Instructions:

1. Garlic and shallots Must be sautéed in a little cooking oil in a pot up to fragrant.
2. Combine the ground cumin, coriander, and turmeric. Cook for an additional min.
3. Add the beef chunks and brown them in the pan.
4. Add beef broth, lemongrass, and kaffir lime leaves. After bringing to a boil, lower heat to a simmer. Cook the beef for 1.5 to 2 hrs, or up to it is tender.
5. Take off the kaffir lime and lemongrass leaves from the pot.
6. To the soup, add potatoes and carrots. Cook the vegetables up to they are soft.
7. Add salt and pepper to the soup to season it.
8. Serve the soup in dishes with bean sprouts, a hard-boiled egg slice in half, fried shallots, and cilantro that has been chop-up.

Nutrition (per serving):
Cals: 300, Protein: 20g
Fat: 12g, Carbs: 25g, Fiber: 4g

97. Pukis (Sweet Filled Pancake)

Prep Time: 15 mins

Cook Time: 20 mins

Total Time: 35 mins

Servings: 12

Ingredients:

- 1 cup of all-purpose flour
- 1/2 cup of coconut milk
- 1/2 cup of milk
- 1/4 cup of granulated sugar
- 2 eggs
- 1/2 tsp baking powder
- 1/4 tsp salt
- 1/2 tsp vanilla extract
- Filling of your choice: chocolate chips, cheese, jam, etc.

Instructions:

1. Combine the salt, baking powder, and flour in a bowl.
2. Eggs and sugar Must be thoroughly combined and somewhat frothy in a separate bowl.
3. Add vanilla extract, normal milk, and coconut milk to the egg Mixture. Combine thoroughly.
4. Stirring occasionally, add the dry ingredients in mini amounts to the wet components. Avoid overcombining; a few lumps are acceptable.
5. Over medium-low heat, preheat a pukis pan or a standard pancake pan. If using a pan for pukis, lightly oil the molds.
6. Fill every mold halfway with batter by adding a mini quantity to it.
7. Put a little amount of filling (such as cheese or chocolate chips) in the middle of every mold.
8. Add a bit extra batter on top, totally encasing the contents.
9. Cook for a few mins, or up to the bottom is golden brown and the edges are set. Make a gentle flip of every puki using a tiny spatula or skewer.
10. Cook for a few more mins, or up to the filling is dilute and the opposite side is golden brown.
11. Before serving, take the pukis out of the pan and let them cool somewhat.

Nutrition (per serving, without filling):
Cals: 90, Protein: 3g
Fat: 3g, Carbs: 13g, Fiber: 0.5g

98. Nasi Kebuli (Arabian-style Rice)

Prep Time: 30 mins

Cook Time: 40 mins

Total Time: 1 hr 10 mins

Servings: 6

Ingredients:

- 2 cups of basmati rice, washed and soaked
- 500g lamb or chicken, slice into pieces
- 2 onions, thinly split
- 3 cloves garlic, chop-up
- 2 tsp ground cumin
- 2 tsp ground coriander
- 1 tsp ground turmeric
- 1/2 tsp ground cinnamon
- 1/4 tsp ground nutmeg

- 1/4 tsp ground cardamom
- 1/4 tsp ground cloves
- 1/4 cup of ghee or butter
- 4 cups of chicken broth
- 1/2 cup of raisins
- 1/2 cup of toasted almonds
- Salt and pepper as needed

Instructions:

1. Butter or ghee Must be heated over medium heat in a big pot. Split onions Must be cooked up to golden.
2. Once aromatic, add the chop-up garlic and continue to cook for another min.
3. Once the lamb or chicken pieces are added, sauté them up to both sides are browned.
4. Add ground cloves, nutmeg, cinnamon, nutcracker, nutmeg, coriander, turmeric, and cumin. Combine well to evenly distribute the spices over the meat.
5. Stir in the soaked rice after adding it to the saucepan with the meat and seasonings.
6. Add the chicken broth and salt and pepper as needed. up to a boil.
7. When the rice is done and the liquid has been absorbed, turn the heat down to low, cover the pot, and let the rice simmer for 20 to 25 mins.
8. Prepare the raisins by soaking them in warm water for a short period of time to plump them up while the rice is cooking.
9. With a fork, fluff the cooked rice after it has been added the raisins that have been soaked.
10. Serve the nasi kebuli with roasted almonds as a garnish.

Nutrition (per serving):
Cals: 450, Protein: 20g

Fat: 15g, Carbs: 60g, Fiber: 3g

99.Tumis Daun Singkong (Stir-fried Cassava Leaves)

Prep Time: 15 mins

Cook Time: 20 mins

Total Time: 35 mins

Servings: 4

Ingredients:

- 300 grams cassava leaves, cleaned and chop-up
- 150 grams shrimp. peel off and deveined
- 2 cloves garlic, chop-up
- 2 shallots, split
- 2 red chili peppers, split
- 1 tomato, chop-up
- 1 tbsp cooking oil
- Salt as needed

Instructions:

1. In a pan, heat the cooking oil on medium.
2. Garlic and shallots are sautéed up to aromatic.
3. Cook the shrimp, stirring occasionally, up to pink.
4. Add the tomato and red chili peppers, and stir-fry for one min.
5. Add the cassava leaves and cook them up to they are wilted.
6. Salt as needed and season as desired.
7. As a side dish, serve warm.

Nutrition (per serving):
Cals: 120 kcal, Protein: 8g

Carbs: 10g

Fat: 5g, Fiber: 3g

100. Lontong Cap Go Meh (Rice Cake with Sweet Gravy)

Prep Time: 1 hr (including soaking time)

Cook Time: 2 hrs

Total Time: 3 hrs

Servings: 6

Ingredients:

- 300 grams glutinous rice, soaked for 1 hr and drained
- 2 lemongrass stalks, bruised
- 4 kaffir lime leaves
- 400 ml coconut milk
- 1 tsp salt
- 1 tsp sugar
- 500 ml sweet gravy (made from palm sugar, water, and pandan leaves)
- Banana leaves, slice into squares and heated to soften

Instructions:

1. In a pot, combine the glutinous rice that has been soaked with the coconut milk, lemongrass, kaffir lime leaves, salt, and sugar.
2. Stirring often, boil the Mixture over low heat up to the rice is done and the coconut milk has been absorbed.
3. Take a piece of banana leaf, place some cooked glutinous rice in the middle, then roll the leaf up into a cylinder. Use toothpicks to fasten the ends.
4. The wrapped rice cakes Must steam for 30 to 40 mins to become done.
5. Serve the sweet gravy beside the steaming rice cakes.

Nutrition (per serving):
Cals: 320 kcal, Protein: 3g

Carbs: 60g, Fat: 8g, Fiber: 1g

101. Sambal Bajak (Combined Chili Sauce)

Prep Time: 15 mins

Cook Time: 10 mins

Total Time: 25 mins

Servings: 8

Ingredients:

- 5 red chili peppers, seeded and split
- 5 bird's eye chili peppers, split
- 3 cloves garlic
- 2 shallots
- 1 tsp shrimp paste (terasi)
- 1 tsp palm sugar or brown sugar
- 1 tsp tamarind paste
- Salt as needed

Instructions:

1. In a mixer, puree shrimp paste, red chili peppers, bird's eye chili peppers, garlic, and shallots.
2. The blended chili Mixture Must be added to a pan that is already hot.
3. Cook up to aromatic for a few mins.
4. Add salt, tamarind paste, and palm sugar. Cook and stir the ingredients up to they are well-balanced.
5. Before serving, take out from the heat and let it cool.

Nutrition (per serving):

Cals: 20 kcal, Protein: 1g

Carbs: 4g, Fat: 0g, Fiber: 1g

102. Pepes Ikan Tongkol (Mackerel Fish in Banana Leaves)

Prep Time: 30 mins

Cook Time: 30 mins

Total Time: 1 hr

Servings: 4

Ingredients:

- 4 mackerel fish steaks
- Banana leaves, slice into rectangles and heated to soften
- 2 tomatoes, split
- 2 lemongrass stalks, bruised
- 4 kaffir lime leaves
- Salt as needed
- For the Spice Paste:
- 4 shallots
- 3 cloves garlic
- 3 red chili peppers (adjust to your spice preference)
- 2 candlenuts or macadamia nuts
- 1 tsp turmeric powder
- 1 tsp coriander powder
- 1 tsp salt

Instructions:

1. The spice paste ingredients Must be processed in a mixer up to smooth.
2. Making sure the fish steaks are thoroughly covered, combine the spice paste with them. For 15 to 20 mins, marinate.
3. On a banana leaf, arrange a fish steak and garnish with tomato slices, lemongrass, and kaffir lime leaves.
4. To contain the fish, fold the banana leaf, then fasten it with toothpicks.
5. Up to the fish is done, steam the sealed fish packets for about 25 to 30 mins.
6. Serve rice beside the fish pouches.

Nutrition (per serving):

Cals: 250 kcal, Protein: 25g

Carbs: 5g

Fat: 15g, Fiber: 1g

103. Kue Lapis Legit (Layered Spice Cake)

Prep Time: 1 hr

Cook Time: 1 hr

Total Time: 2 hrs

Servings: 16 slices

Ingredients:

- 500g butter, melted
- 250g condensed milk
- 200g granulated sugar
- 12 egg yolks
- 150g all-purpose flour
- 1 tsp ground cinnamon
- 1/2 tsp ground nutmeg
- 1/2 tsp ground cloves
- 1/2 tsp vanilla extract
- Pinch of salt

Instructions:

1. Set your oven's temperature to 180 °C (350 °F). An 8-inch square baking pan Must be greased and lined.
2. Cream the butter, condensed milk, and sugar in a sizable basin up to it turns light and fluffy.
3. One at a time, gradually add the egg yolks, combining well after every addition.
4. The flour Must be sifted in and gradually incorporated into the batter.
5. Make two pieces of the batter. Combine thoroughly after adding the vanilla extract and spices to one portion.

6. In the pan that has been prepared, spread a thin layer of the spiced batter, and bake for about 10 mins, or up to firm.
7. Layer plain and spiced batter alternately, bake every layer up to set, and repeat up to all of the batter has been used.
8. Take out the cake from the oven and let it to cool in the pan once it has finished baking and the layers are golden brown.
9. Slice the cake into thin slices and serve once it has totally cooled.

Nutrition (per slice):

Cals: 280, Fat: 18g

Carbs: 25g

Protein: 4g

104. Pecel Madiun (Madiun-style Salad with Peanut Sauce)

Prep Time: 30 mins

Cook Time: 15 mins

Total Time: 45 mins

Servings: 4

Ingredients:
- 300g combined vegetables (cabbage, long beans, bean sprouts, cucumber, etc.)
- 200g rice cakes (lontong), slice into bite-sized pieces
- 100g tempeh, thinly split and fried
- 100g tofu, fried and cubed
- 100g peanut sauce (you can make it using ground peanuts, tamarind, palm sugar, and spices)

Instructions:
1. On a serving platter, arrange the fried tofu, fried tempeh, fried tempeh cakes, and combined vegetables.
2. Over the rice cakes and vegetables, drizzle the peanut sauce.
3. Before eating, combine everything and serve immediately.

Nutrition (per serving):

Cals: 350, Fat: 20g

Carbs: 30g

Protein: 15g

105. Tahu Campur Surabaya (Surabaya-style Tofu Salad)

Prep Time: 20 mins

Cook Time: 15 mins

Total Time: 35 mins

Servings: 4

Ingredients:
- 300g firm tofu, cubed
- 100g bean sprouts
- 1 cucumber, thinly split
- 2 boiled eggs, halved
- 2 shallots, thinly split
- 2 cloves garlic, chop-up
- 2 red chilies, split
- 1 cup of shrimp, peel off and deveined
- 1 cup of cabbage, shredded
- 1 cup of water spinach (kangkung), slice into 2-inch pieces
- 2 tbsp tamarind juice
- 2 tbsp sweet soy sauce
- Salt and sugar as needed
- Cooking oil

Instructions:
1. Tofu cubes are fried in hot oil up to golden brown. Take out, then dry off with paper towels.
2. Garlic and shallots Must be sautéed in the same pan up to aromatic.
3. When the shrimp are pink, add them and continue to boil. Take out and place aside.
4. The water spinach and cabbage Must be stir-fried up to wilted. Take out and place aside.
5. To make the dressing, combine tamarind juice, sweet soy sauce, salt, and sugar in a bowl.
6. Place the boiled eggs, cucumber, bean sprouts, shrimp, fried tofu, and other veggies on a platter.
7. Add the red chile slices as a garnish after dressing the salad.
8. Steamed rice Must be served with Tahu Campur Surabaya.

Nutrition (per serving):

Cals: 280, Protein: 18g

Carbs: 20g

Fat: 14g, Fiber: 4g

106. Nasi Langgi (Rice with Various Side Dishes)

Prep Time: 30 mins

Cook Time: 40 mins

Total Time: 1 hr 10 mins

Servings: 6

Ingredients:
- 3 cups of white rice, cooked and cooled
- 200g tempeh, thinly split and fried
- 200g tofu, fried and cubed
- 150g shredded coconut, toasted
- 4 hard-boiled eggs, halved
- 100g crispy fried shallots

- 1 cup of green beans, blanched and split
- 1 cup of cucumber, split
- 1 cup of carrot, julienned
- 1 cup of fried chicken pieces
- Sweet soy sauce and chili sauce for serving
- Banana leaves for serving

Instructions:
1. Place some cooked rice in a mound on a piece of banana leaf.
2. Top the rice with the fried chicken, tempeh, tofu, coconut flakes, crispy fried shallots, green beans, cucumber, and carrot.
3. Serve with cooked eggs, sweet soy sauce, and chili sauce as toppings.
4. For every serving, repeat the procedure.
5. To create a tidy gift, wrap the rice and side dishes in banana leaves.
6. The nasi langgi is prepared for serving.

Nutrition (per serving):
Cals: 480, Protein: 14g

Carbs: 50g

Fat: 26g, Fiber: 3g

107. Otak-Otak (Spiced Fish Cake)

Prep Time: 20 mins

Cook Time: 20 mins

Total Time: 40 mins

Servings: 4

Ingredients:
- 500g white fish fillets (such as snapper or mackerel), deboned and lightly chop-up
- 2 tbsp red curry paste
- 1 egg
- 1/4 cup of coconut milk
- 2 kaffir lime leaves, lightly split
- 1 tbsp fish sauce
- 1 tsp sugar
- Banana leaves, slice into 4 squares for wrapping
- Bamboo skewers, soaked in water

Instructions:
1. The chop-up fish, red curry paste, egg, coconut milk, kaffir lime leaves, fish sauce, and sugar Must all be combined in a combining bowl. Combine thoroughly up to everything is well-combined.
2. Place some of the fish Mixture in the center of a square of banana leaf. To enclose the Mixture, fold the leaf, and then fasten it with bamboo skewers.

3. Over medium heat, grill the wrapped fish cakes for about 10 mins on every side, or up to fully cooked and moderately browned.
4. Otak-otak Must be served hot with steamed rice.

NUTRITION INFO: (per serving)
Cals: 220 kcal, Protein: 20g

Fat: 12g, Carbs: 9g, Fiber: 1g

108. Laksa Betawi (Betawi Noodle Soup)

Prep Time: 15 mins

Cook Time: 30 mins

Total Time: 45 mins

Servings: 6

Ingredients:
- 200g rice noodles, soaked in hot water up to soft
- 200g cooked shrimp, peel off and deveined
- 200g cooked chicken breast, shredded
- 4 boiled eggs, halved
- 400ml coconut milk
- 1 liter chicken or beef broth
- 2 tbsp cooking oil
- 2 tbsp tamarind juice
- 2 tbsp sweet soy sauce
- 2 cloves garlic, chop-up
- 1 onion, chop-up
- 1 tbsp ground coriander
- 1 tsp ground turmeric
- 1 tsp shrimp paste
- Salt and sugar as needed
- Bean sprouts, chop-up fresh herbs, and lime wedges for serving

Instructions:
1. Cooking oil Must be heated in a sizable pot over medium heat. The onion and garlic are chop-up, and they are cooked up to aromatic.
2. Add the shrimp paste, ground turmeric, and coriander. Stir-fry up to fragrant for one min.
3. Add the chicken or beef broth, then boil the Mixture. Add the tamarind juice, sweet soy sauce, and coconut milk. As needed, add salt and sugar to the dish.
4. Divide the melted rice noodles among serving bowls before serving. Add cooked shrimp, chop-up chicken, and boiled eggs in halves as garnish.
5. Over the noodles and garnishes, ladle the heated soup.
6. Lime wedges, bean sprouts, and lightly chop-up fresh herbs are garnishes.

NUTRITION INFO: (per serving)
Cals: 420 kcal, Protein: 22g

Fat: 20g, Carbs: 40g

Fiber: 3g

109. Gulai Kambing (Lamb Curry)

Prep Time: 20 mins

Cook Time: 1 hr 30 mins

Total Time: 1 hr 50 mins

Servings: 4

Ingredients:

- 800g lamb meat, slice into chunks
- 2 onions, lightly chop-up
- 3 cloves garlic, chop-up
- 2 tbsp ginger paste
- 2 tbsp curry powder
- 1 tsp turmeric powder
- 1 tsp coriander powder
- 1 tsp cumin powder
- 4 cardamom pods
- 2 cloves
- 2 stalks lemongrass, bruised
- 4 kaffir lime leaves
- 400ml coconut milk
- 500ml water
- 2 tbsp cooking oil
- Salt and sugar as needed
- Chop-up cilantro for garnish

Instructions:

1. Cooking oil Must be heated in a sizable pot over medium heat. Once the onions are transparent, add the chop-up garlic and ginger Mixture to the pan.
2. Add the lamb chunks and continue cooking them up to they are evenly browned.
3. Add the cumin, coriander, curry, and turmeric powders after stirring. Cook up to aromatic for a few of mins.
4. Add the cloves, lemongrass, cardamom pods, and kaffir lime leaves. Add the water and coconut milk. Simmer for a while.
5. Once the lamb is cooked, let the curry simmer on low heat for about an hr covered.
6. Add salt and sugar as needed when preparing the curry. Simmer for a further ten mins.
7. Before serving, garnish with chop-up cilantro.

NUTRITION INFO: (per serving)
Cals: 550 kcal, Protein: 32g, Fat: 40g

Carbs: 12g, Fiber: 2g

110. Papeda Kuah Ikan (Sago Porridge with Fish Soup)

Prep Time: 10 mins

Cook Time: 30 mins

Total Time: 40 mins

Servings: 4

Ingredients:

- 200g sago pearls
- 400g white fish fillets, slice into chunks
- 1 liter fish or seafood broth
- 2 cloves garlic, chop-up
- 2 shallots, lightly chop-up
- 2 red chilies, split
- 1 tomato, chop-up
- 2 kaffir lime leaves
- 1 stalk lemongrass, bruised
- Salt and sugar as needed
- Chop-up fresh herbs for garnish

Instructions:

1. Sago pearls Must be rinsed with cold water. Sago pearls are put in a kettle of boiling water. Cook the pearls for 15 to 20 mins, or up to they become translucent. Drain, then set apart.
2. Heat some oil in a different pot, add the chop-up garlic, shallots, and red chilies, and cook up to fragrant.
3. Cook the fish chunks after adding them up to they begin to get opaque.
4. Along with the chop-up tomato, kaffir lime leaves, and lemongrass, pour in the fish or seafood broth. For around 15 mins, let the soup boil.
5. Add sugar and salt as needed when preparing the soup.
6. Sago pearls that have been cooked Must go in every bowl before the hot fish soup is added.
7. Before serving, garnish with lightly chop-up fresh herbs.

NUTRITION INFO: (per serving)
Cals: 280 kcal, Protein: 20g

Fat: 6g, Carbs: 35g, Fiber: 2g

111.Lontong Kari (Rice Cake in Curry)

Prep Time: 30 mins

Cook Time: 1 hr

Total Time: 1 hr 30 mins

Servings: 4

Ingredients:

- 2 cups of rice, soaked and drained
- Banana leaves, slice into squares
- 1 chicken breast, boiled and shredded
- 1 cup of coconut milk
- 2 cups of water
- 2 tbsp curry powder
- 1 tsp turmeric powder

- Salt as needed
- Fried shallots, for garnish

Instructions:
1. To create little pouches for the rice, slice the banana leaves into squares.
2. Every pouch Must be filled with moistened rice before being steamed up to done and compact.
3. Coconut milk, water, salt, curry powder, and turmeric powder Must all be combined in a pot. Simmer for a while.
4. Stir in the chicken shreds and boil the curry sauce for 10 to 15 mins.
5. Serve the chicken curry on top of the steamed rice cakes (lontong).
6. Before serving, add fried shallots as a garnish.

Nutrition (per serving):
Cals: 450, Protein: 15g

Carbs: 60g

Fat: 18g, Fiber: 2g

112. Sate Kambing Betawi (Betawi-style Lamb Satay)

Prep Time: 45 mins

Cook Time: 15 mins

Total Time: 1 hr

Servings: 6

Ingredients:
- 1 lb lamb meat, slice into mini cubes
- 1 tbsp vegetable oil
- 3 cloves garlic, chop-up
- 1 tsp coriander powder
- 1 tsp cumin powder
- Salt and pepper as needed
- Bamboo skewers, soaked in water

Instructions:
1. Combine the vegetable oil, chop-up garlic, cumin, coriander, salt, and pepper in a bowl.
2. Include the lamb cubes in the marinade and thoroughly coat them. Give it at least 30 mins to marinate.
3. Bamboo skewers that have been steeped in marinade are threaded with lamb cubes.
4. If using a grill pan, roast the skewers for 5 to 7 mins on every side, or up to the lamb is cooked to the desired doneness.
5. Rice and peanut sauce Must be served with the lamb satay.

Nutrition (per serving):
Cals: 220, Protein: 18g

Carbs: 2g, Fat: 16g, Fiber: 1g

113. Serabi Solo (Solo-style Coconut Pancakes)

Prep Time: 15 mins

Cook Time: 20 mins

Total Time: 35 mins

Servings: 4

Ingredients:
- 1 cup of rice flour
- 1/4 cup of all-purpose flour
- 1 cup of coconut milk
- 1/2 cup of water
- 1/4 tsp salt
- 2 tbsp granulated sugar
- Pandan leaves or pandan extract (non-compulsory, for flavor)
- Finely grated coconut, steamed, for topping
- Palm sugar syrup, for topping

Instructions:
1. Rice flour, all-purpose flour, coconut milk, water, salt, and sugar Must be thoroughly combined in a bowl.
2. In order to add flavor to the batter when using pandan leaves, combine the leaves with a little water and drain the juice.
3. A nonstick pan Must be heated to medium. To make a pancake, spoon some batter onto the pan.
4. Cook up to surface mini holes emerge, then cover the pan and continue cooking for an additional min or up to the pancake is thoroughly done.
5. With the remaining batter, repeat the procedure.
6. Finely grated coconut and palm sugar syrup Must be drizzled over the coconut pancakes before serving.

Nutrition (per serving):
Cals: 250, Protein: 2g

Carbs: 40g

Fat: 9g, Fiber: 1g

114. Tahu Campur Surabaya (Surabaya-style Tofu Salad)

Prep Time: 20 mins

Cook Time: 15 mins

Total Time: 35 mins

Servings: 4

Ingredients:
- 1 block firm tofu, slice into cubes
- 1 cup of bean sprouts

- 1 cucumber, julienned
- 1 mini carrot, julienned
- 2 boiled eggs, halved
- Shrimp crackers, for garnish
- Fried shallots, for garnish

Instructions:

1. The tofu cubes Must be fried up to crisp and golden. On paper towels, drain.
2. The bean sprouts Must be briefly blanched in boiling water before being immediately rinsed in cold water and drained.
3. On a serving platter, arrange the fried tofu, blanched bean sprouts, cucumber, carrot, and boiled eggs.
4. Add fried shallots on top and serve with shrimp crackers.
5. Choose whether to drizzle with sweet soy sauce or peanut sauce.

Nutrition (per serving):

Cals: 280, Protein: 14g

Carbs: 15g

Fat: 18g, Fiber: 3g

115. Kue Cucur (Fried Pancake with Palm Sugar)

Prep Time: 15 mins

Cook Time: 20 mins

Total Time: 35 mins

Servings: 4

Ingredients:

- 1 cup of rice flour
- 1/4 cup of all-purpose flour
- 1/4 tsp salt
- 1 tsp baking powder
- 3/4 cup of coconut milk
- 1/2 cup of water
- Palm sugar, finely grated or chop-up
- Oil for frying

Instructions:

1. Combine rice flour, all-purpose flour, baking powder, salt, and a bowl.
2. Water and coconut milk Must be added gradually to the dry ingredients. Combine up to a smooth batter is obtained.
3. In a frying pan, heat the oil over medium-low heat.
4. A tiny ladleful of batter Must be poured into the pan to create a circle.
5. In the middle of the batter, add a tiny amount of palm sugar that has been shredded or diced.

6. More batter Must be used to cover the palm sugar.
7. Fry up to both sides are golden brown. Eliminate and absorb extra oil on paper towels.

Nutrition (per serving):

Cals: Approximately 200 kcal, Carbs: 30g

Fat: 6g, Protein: 2g

116. Bubur Sumsum Hijau (Green Rice Porridge with Palm Sugar)

Prep Time: 10 mins

Cook Time: 30 mins

Total Time: 40 mins

Servings: 6

Ingredients:

- 1 cup of glutinous rice flour
- 4 cups of coconut milk
- 1/2 tsp salt
- Pandan leaves, tied into a knot (for flavor and color)
- Palm sugar, finely grated or chop-up

Instructions:

1. Coconut milk and glutinous rice flour Must be well combined in a pot.
2. To the Mixture, add salt and pandan leaves.
3. Stirring continuously, cook the Mixture over medium heat up to it reverges the consistency of porridge.
4. Take away the pandan leaves.
5. The porridge Must be served in bowls with finely grated or chop-up palm sugar on top.

Nutrition (per serving):

Cals: Approximately 250 kcal, Carbs: 30g

Fat: 14g, Protein: 2g

117. Klepon Ketan Putih (White Glutinous Rice Cake with Palm Sugar)

Prep Time: 30 mins

Cook Time: 20 mins

Total Time: 50 mins

Servings: 12

Ingredients:

- 2 cups of glutinous rice flour
- About 1 cup of hot water
- Palm sugar, slice into mini cubes
- Finely grated coconut, steamed and combined with a pinch of salt

Instructions:

1. Add hot water gradually while stirring a bowl of

glutinous rice flour. Up up to you have a smooth, malleable dough, combine and knead.

2. A mini amount of the dough Must be flattened in your palm.
3. Wrap the dough around a cube of palm sugar in the center, creating a ball.
4. the remaining dough with palm sugar, then repeat.
5. Water is being heated in a pot. Enter the boiling water with the rice balls. When they float to the top, they are finished.
6. The rice balls Must be taken out of the water and covered with finely grated coconut.

Nutrition (per serving):
Cals: Approximately 150 kcal, Carbs: 25g

Fat: 5g, Protein: 2g

118. Tumis Kangkung Bawang Putih (Stir-fried Water Spinach with Garlic)

Prep Time: 10 mins

Cook Time: 5 mins

Total Time: 15 mins

Servings: 4

Ingredients:
- 1 bunch water spinach (kangkung), washed and slice into 2-inch lengths
- 3 cloves garlic, chop-up
- 2 tbsp cooking oil
- 1 tsp soy sauce
- Salt and pepper as needed

Instructions:
1. In a wok or frying pan, heat the oil over medium-high heat.
2. Sauté the garlic up to it is aromatic and just beginning to turn golden.
3. Water spinach Must be added to the skillet and stir-fried up to wilted for a few mins.
4. Add soy sauce, salt, and pepper for seasoning. Combine thoroughly by tossing.
5. Transfer to a serving dish after taking it off the heat.

Nutrition (per serving):
Cals: Approximately 50 kcal, Carbs: 4g

Fat: 3g, Protein: 2g

119. Tumis Kangkung Bawang Putih (Stir-fried Water Spinach with Garlic)

Prep Time: 10 mins

Cook Time: 5 mins

Total Time: 15 mins

Servings: 4

Ingredients:
- 300 grams water spinach (kangkung), washed and slice into 2-inch pieces
- 3 cloves garlic, chop-up
- 2 tbsp cooking oil
- 1 tsp soy sauce
- Salt and pepper as needed

Instructions:
1. In a wok or pan, heat the cooking oil over medium-high heat.
2. Sauté the garlic up to it is fragrant and yellow after being added.
3. Water spinach Must be added to the wok and stir-fried for 2 to 3 mins, or up to the leaves are wilted.
4. After one more min of stirring, drizzle soy sauce over the water spinach.
5. As needed, add salt and pepper to the food.
6. Transfer to a serving dish after taking it off the heat.
7. As a side dish with rice or as a main course, serve the Tumis Kangkung.

NUTRITION INFO (per serving):
Cals: 60 kcal, Protein: 2g

Fat: 4g, Carbs: 5g, Fiber: 2g

120. Lontong Kari (Rice Cake in Curry)

Prep Time: 20 mins

Cook Time: 1 hr

Total Time: 1 hr 20 mins

Servings: 6

Ingredients:
- 400 grams rice cakes (lontong), slice into bite-sized pieces
- 200 grams chicken, beef, or vegetables (your choice), cooked and diced
- 400 ml coconut milk
- 2 tbsp curry powder
- 1 onion, lightly chop-up
- 3 cloves garlic, chop-up
- 2 tbsp cooking oil
- Salt and sugar as needed
- Non-compulsory toppings: fried shallots, chop-up cilantro

Instructions:
1. Over medium heat, warm the cooking oil in the pot. Sauté the chop-up garlic and onion up to aromatic.
2. To release its flavors, add the curry powder and heat for a min.

3. Add the coconut milk, then boil the Mixture. Cook it for about five mins.
4. To the curry, add the cooked chicken, meat, or veggies. As needed, add salt and sugar to the dish.
5. Add the rice cake pieces to the curry and give them 10 to 15 mins to absorb the spices.
6. Take out from heat once the rice cakes are tender and the curry has thickened.
7. If preferred, top the Lontong Kari with chop-up cilantro and fried shallots when serving.

NUTRITION INFO (per serving):
Cals: 350 kcal, Protein: 10g

Fat: 25g, Carbs: 26g

Fiber: 3g

121. Sate Kambing Betawi (Betawi-style Lamb Satay)

Prep Time: 30 mins

Cook Time: 15 mins

Total Time: 45 mins

Servings: 4

Ingredients:
- 500 grams lamb meat, slice into cubes
- 1 onion, finely grated
- 2 cloves garlic, chop-up
- 1 tsp ground coriander
- 1 tsp ground cumin
- 1/2 tsp turmeric
- 1 tbsp sweet soy sauce (kecap manis)
- Salt and pepper as needed
- Bamboo skewers, soaked in water

Instructions:
1. To make a marinace, combine the lightly chop-up garlic, ground coriander, ground cumin, ground turmeric, sweet soy sauce, salt, and pepper in a basin.
2. Include the lamb cubes in the marinade and thoroughly coat them. Give the meat at least 15 to 30 mins to marinade.
3. Bamboo skewers that have been steeped in marinade are threaded with lamb cubes.
4. As the meat cooks to the appropriate doneness, grill or roast the skewers on a barbecue or grill pan for around 8 to 10 mins.
5. Sate Kambing Betawi Must be served hot with rice and peanut sauce.

NUTRITION INFO (per serving):
Cals: 280 kcal, Protein: 25g

Fat: 18g, Carbs: 4g

Fiber: 1g

122. Serabi Solo (Solo-style Coconut Pancakes)

Prep Time: 15 mins

Cook Time: 20 mins

Total Time: 35 mins

Servings: 4

Ingredients:
- 200 grams rice flour
- 50 grams all-purpose flour
- 400 ml coconut milk
- 100 ml water
- 100 grams granulated sugar
- 1/2 tsp salt
- Banana slices, chocolate sprinkles, or finely grated coconut (for topping)
- Oil for greasing the pan

Instructions:
1. Rice flour, all-purpose flour, coconut milk, water, sugar, and salt Must all be combined in a combining bowl. Combine thoroughly and blend up to smooth.
2. Let the batter to sit for ten to fifteen mins.
3. A nonstick pan Must be heated over medium heat while being gently greased with oil.
4. To make a thin pancake, pour a mini amount of batter into the pan. To uniformly distribute the batter, swirl the pan.
5. Cook the pancake up to the surface is dry and the edges begin to lift
6. If desired, garnish the pancake with finely grated coconut, banana segments, or chocolate shavings.
7. The pancake Must be faintly golden on both sides after you fold it in half and cook it for another min.
8. With the remaining batter, repeat the procedure.
9. Serabi Solo is a delicious Indonesian dessert or snack that is best served warm.

NUTRITION INFO (per serving, without toppings):
Cals: 300 kcal, Protein: 3g

Fat: 12g, Carbs: 45g, Fiber: 1g

123.Nasi Langgi (Rice with Various Side Dishes)

Prep Time: 30 mins

Cook Time: 40 mins

Total Time: 1 hr 10 mins

Servings: 4

Ingredients:

- 2 cups of white rice, washed and drained
- 4 cups of water
- 1 tsp salt
- 1 cup of shredded coconut, steamed
- 4 boiled eggs, halved
- 1 cup of fried tempeh, split
- 1 cup of fried tofu, split
- 1 cup of fried anchovies
- 1 cup of sautéed spinach with garlic
- 1 cup of sambal (spicy chili paste)
- Banana leaves for serving

Instructions:

1. Combine the washed rice, water, and salt in a rice cooker. Rice Must be prepared as directed by the rice cooker.
2. With a fork, fluff the cooked rice and keep it warm.
3. On a sizable serving tray covered with banana leaves, arrange the cooked rice, lightly chop-up coconut, boiled eggs, fried tempeh, fried tofu, fried anchovies, sautéed spinach, and sambal.
4. Enjoy the Nasi Langgi along with the side dishes!

Nutrition (per serving):
Cals: 450 kcal, Carbs: 60g

Protein: 12g, Fat: 18g, Fiber: 5g

124. Kue Cucur (Fried Pancake with Palm Sugar)

Prep Time: 15 mins

Cook Time: 20 mins

Total Time: 35 mins

Servings: 6

Ingredients:

- 1 cup of rice flour
- ¼ cup of all-purpose flour
- ½ tsp salt
- ½ tsp turmeric powder
- 1 tsp baking powder
- ¾ cup of water
- ½ cup of coconut milk
- Oil for frying
- Palm sugar (gula jawa) for filling

Instructions:

1. Rice flour, all-purpose flour, salt, turmeric powder, and baking powder Must all be combined in a bowl.
2. When a smooth batter formed, gradually add water and coconut milk to the dry ingredients while stirring.

3. In a frying pan, heat the oil over medium-low heat.
4. Pour a tiny amount of batter into the pan and spread it out into a circle using a ladle.
5. Place a mini bit of palm sugar in the center and cover with a little more batter after cooking up to surface bubbles appear.
6. Fry up to golden brown on both sides.
7. Replicate the process with the remaining batter and palm sugar.
8. To drain off extra oil, place the fried pancakes on paper towels.
9. Kue Cucur Must be served warm.

Nutrition (per serving, without palm sugar):
Cals: 150 kcal, Carbs: 30g

Protein: 2g, Fat: 1g, Fiber: 1g

125. Bubur Sumsum Hijau (Green Rice Porridge with Palm Sugar)

Prep Time: 5 mins

Cook Time: 30 mins

Total Time: 35 mins

Servings: 4

Ingredients:

- ½ cup of glutinous rice flour
- 2 pandan leaves, knotted
- 4 cups of water
- ½ cup of palm sugar, finely grated
- ½ cup of coconut milk
- A pinch of salt
- Toasted sesame seeds for garnish

Instructions:

1. Combine glutinous rice flour and a mini amount of water in a bowl to create a smooth paste.
2. Add the pandan leaves to 4 cups of boiling water in a kettle.
3. Pour the paste made from glutinous rice flour in gradually, stirring constantly to avoid lumps.
4. Cook the Mixture up to it thickens into a smooth porridge over medium heat.
5. Add a dash of salt and the coconut milk along with the palm sugar. Stir thoroughly up to cooked all the way through.
6. Pandan leaves must be take outd.
7. Bubur Sumsum Hijau Must be served in bowls with toasted sesame seeds on top.

Nutrition (per serving):
Cals: 180 kcal, Carbs: 30g

Protein: 1g, Fat: 7g, Fiber: 1g

126. Klepon Ketan Putih (White Glutinous Rice Cake with Palm Sugar)

Prep Time: 30 mins

Cook Time: 20 mins

Total Time: 50 mins

Servings: 12

Ingredients:

- 2 cups of glutinous rice flour
- ½ cup of hot water
- Palm sugar (gula jawa), slice into mini cubes
- Finely grated coconut, steamed and combined with a pinch of salt, for coating

Instructions:

1. Combine the boiling water and glutinous rice flour in a bowl up to a smooth dough forms.
2. A mini amount of the dough Must be flattened in your palm.
3. Wrap the dough around a cube of palm sugar in the center to create a tiny ball.
4. the remaining dough with palm sugar, then repeat.
5. Water Must be heated up in a pot.
6. Rice balls Must be carefully dropped into hot water and cooked up to they float to the top.
7. Take out the rice balls from the water using a slotted spoon, then quickly coat them in the finely grated coconut.
8. Before serving, let the Klepon Ketan Putih to cool somewhat.

Nutrition (per serving):

Cals: 100 kcal, Carbs: 22g

Protein: 1g, Fat: 2g, Fiber: 1g

127. Lontong Medan (Medan-style Rice Cake)

Prep Time: 30 mins

Cook Time: 2 hrs

Total Time: 2 hrs 30 mins

Servings: 6

Ingredients:

- 2 cups of rice, soaked and drained
- Banana leaves, slice into 6-inch squares
- Water for boiling
- Salt, as needed

Instructions:

1. Use a mixer or a mortar and pestle to pulverize the soaked and dried rice into a fine pulp.
2. The rice paste Must be combined with a mini amount of salt.
3. Fold a square of banana leaf into a cone form, and then fasten the edges using toothpicks.
4. The rice paste Must be poured into the banana leaf cone, leaving room at the top for the rice to expand.
5. Place the banana leaf cones that have been filled in a big pot of boiling water. Make sure the cones are submerged in water.
6. The rice cakes Must be boiled for around two hrs, adding water as necessary.
7. Once cooked, take the rice cakes from the water and let them to cool somewhat.
8. Take out the banana leaves from the rice cakes and slice them into rounds.
9. Your choice of sauces and side dishes Must be served with the Lontong Medan.

Nutrition (per serving):

Cals: ~200 kcal

Carbs: ~45g

Protein: ~3g, Fat: ~0g, Fiber: ~1g

128. Es Puter (Coconut Ice Cream)

Prep Time: 20 mins

Cook Time: 10 mins (+ freezing time)

Total Time: 4 hrs

Servings: 4

Ingredients:

- 2 cups of coconut milk
- 3/4 cup of sugar
- 1/4 tsp salt
- 1/2 tsp vanilla extract
- Crushed ice

Instructions:

1. Combine the coconut milk, sugar, and salt in a pot. Stirring occasionally, boil the Mixture over medium heat up to the sugar melts.
2. After turning off the heat, let the Mixture to cool to room temperature.
3. Add the vanilla extract and stir.
4. Fill mini cups of or ice cream molds with the ingredients.
5. For about two hrs, place the molds or cups of in the freezer and let the Mixture to partially freeze.
6. Take the partially refrigerate Mixture out of the freezer and puree it up to smooth.
7. Put the Mixture back into the cups of or molds and freeze for an additional two hrs, or up to solid.
8. Pour the Es Puter into cups of and add crushed ice on top.

Nutrition (per serving):

Cals: ~300 kcal, Carbs: ~30g, Protein: ~2g

Fat: ~20g, Fiber: ~0g

129. Pecel Solo (Solo-style Salad with Peanut Sauce)

Prep Time: 30 mins

Cook Time: 15 mins

Total Time: 45 mins

Servings: 4

Ingredients:

- 4 cups of combined vegetables (cabbage, bean sprouts, long beans, etc.), blanched
- 1 cup of rice vermicelli, cooked and drained
- 1 cup of fried tempeh or tofu, split
- 1/2 cup of peanut sauce (store-bought or homemade)

Instructions:

1. Place the split tempeh or tofu, cooked rice vermicelli, and blanched veggies on serving platters.
2. Sprinkle the vegetables and tempeh/tofu with the peanut sauce.
3. Pecel Solo Must be served right away.

Nutrition (per serving):

Cals: ~350 kcal, Carbs: ~30g

Protein: ~15g, Fat: ~20g, Fiber: ~5g

130. Sate Kerang (Clam Satay)

Prep Time: 1 hr

Cook Time: 10 mins

Total Time: 1 hr 10 mins

Servings: 4

Ingredients:

- 1 lb fresh clams, cleaned and scrubbed
- 1 tbsp vegetable oil
- 1 tbsp sweet soy sauce (kecap manis)
- 1 tsp tamarind paste
- 1 tsp brown sugar
- Skewers, soaked in water

Instructions:

1. To make the marinade, combine the vegetable oil, sweet soy sauce, tamarind paste, and brown sugar in a bowl.
2. The cleaned clams Must be added to the marinade and left to sit for approximately 30 mins.
3. The soaking skewers are then threaded with the marinated clams.
4. Over medium-high heat, preheat a grill or grill pan.

5. The clams Must be cooked and slightly blackened after grilling the clam skewers for two to three mins on every side.
6. With rice and the dipping sauce of your choice, serve the sate kerang hot.

Nutrition (per serving):

Cals: ~150 kcal, Carbs: ~10g

Protein: ~10g, Fat: ~8g, Fiber: ~1g

131. Soto Betawi Makasar (Makasar-style Beef Soup)

Prep Time: 20 mins

Cook Time: 1 hr 30 mins

Total Time: 1 hr 50 mins

Servings: 4

Ingredients:

- 500g beef, slice into chunks
- 1 lemongrass stalk, bruised
- 2 kaffir lime leaves
- 2 bay leaves
- 2 cloves garlic, chop-up
- 1 onion, chop-up
- 1 tsp ground turmeric
- 1 tsp ground coriander
- 1 tsp ground cumin
- Salt and pepper as needed
- 1 liter beef broth
- 400ml coconut milk
- 2 potatoes, peel off and diced
- 2 tomatoes, slice into wedges
- Fried shallots for garnish
- Split green onions for garnish
- Lime wedges for serving

Instructions:

1. Oil Must be heated in a pot before sautéing the garlic and onion up to aromatic.
2. Cook the beef with the spices (cumin, coriander, and turmeric) up to the color changes.
3. Pour the coconut milk and beef broth in. Add bay leaves, lemongrass, and kaffir lime leaves. Simmer the beef up to it is tender.
4. tomato and potato in. Cook the potatoes further up to they are tender.
5. Add salt and pepper as needed.
6. Serve the soup hot, topped with lime wedges, green onions, and fried shallots.

NUTRITION INFO: (per serving)

Cals: 380 kcal, Protein: 20g

Carbs: 20g

Fat: 25g

Fiber: 3g

132. Bubur Ketan Item (Black Glutinous Rice Porridge)

Prep Time: 8 hrs (for soaking rice)

Cook Time: 1 hr

Total Time: 9 hrs

Servings: 6

Ingredients:

- 1 cup of black glutinous rice, soaked overnight
- 5 cups of water
- 400ml coconut milk
- 200g palm sugar, chop-up
- 1/2 tsp salt
- Split ripe bananas for serving
- Finely grated coconut for serving

Instructions:

1. Drain and rinse the soaking sticky rice.
2. Rice and water Must be combined in a pot. Cook the rice up to it is cooked and has absorbed the majority of the water over medium heat.
3. Heat the coconut milk, palm sugar, and salt in a separate pot. As you stir, the palm sugar Must dissolve.
4. To the coconut milk Mixture, include the cooked rice. Stirring regularly, let the porridge simmer on low heat for 15 to 20 mins or up to it thickens.
5. Hot porridge Must be served with finely grated coconut and banana slices on top.

NUTRITION INFO: (per serving)

Cals: 320 kcal, Protein: 3g

Carbs: 63g

Fat: 8g, Fiber: 2g

133. Sambal Kecombrang (Torch Ginger Sambal)

Prep Time: 15 mins

Cook Time: 10 mins

Total Time: 25 mins

Servings: 4

Ingredients:

- 6-8 torch ginger buds (kecombrang), lightly chop-up
- 5 shallots, lightly chop-up
- 3 cloves garlic, chop-up
- 5 red chili peppers, lightly chop-up (adjust for heat)
- 3 bird's eye chili peppers, lightly chop-up (adjust for heat)
- 1 tomato, diced
- 1 tsp shrimp paste (terasi), toasted
- 1 tbsp tamarind paste
- 1 tsp sugar
- Salt as needed
- 2 tbsp vegetable oil

Instructions:

1. Grind the shallots, garlic, red chili peppers, bird's eye chili peppers, and shrimp paste into a smooth paste in a mortar and pestle.
2. Oil in a pan is heated to medium heat. the paste in hot oil up to aromatic.
3. Tomato dice and chop-up torch ginger buds Must be added. The ingredients must be thoroughly blended after a few mins of cooking.
4. Add salt, sugar, and tamarind paste. Stir thoroughly, then cook for a few more mins.
5. If necessary, taste and adjust the seasoning. A combination of spicy, sour, and slightly sweet qualities Must be present in the sambal.
6. Cooked food Must be taken off the heat and leted to cool before serving.

134. Bubur Ketan Merah (Red Glutinous Rice Porridge)

Prep Time: 8 hrs (for soaking rice)

Cook Time: 1 hr

Total Time: 9 hrs

Servings: 6

Ingredients:

- 1 cup of red glutinous rice, soaked overnight
- 5 cups of coconut milk
- 1 pandan leaf, tied in a knot
- 1/2 tsp salt
- Palm sugar or brown sugar, as needed
- Toppings: split bananas, toasted coconut flakes, etc.

Instructions:

1. Drain and rinse the red glutinous rice.
2. Rice, coconut milk, pandan leaf, and salt Must all be combined in a saucepan. Cook for about an hr on low heat, stirring regularly, or up to the rice is tender and the porridge has thickened.
3. Stirring up to dissolved, add palm sugar or brown sugar according as needed.
4. Take the pandan leaf off.
5. Split bananas, toasted coconut flakes, or other preferred toppings may be sprinkled on top of the hot porridge as it is served in bowls.

135. Tahu Gejrot Cirebon (Cirebon-style Fried Tofu)

Prep Time: 15 mins
Cook Time: 15 mins
Total Time: 30 mins
Servings: 4

Ingredients:

- 1 block firm tofu, slice into mini cubes
- 2 shallots, thinly split
- 2 cloves garlic, chop-up
- 2-3 bird's eye chili peppers, chop-up (adjust for heat)
- 1 tsp palm sugar or brown sugar
- 1 tsp tamarind paste
- 1/2 tsp shrimp paste (terasi), toasted
- Salt as needed
- 1 cup of water
- Oil for frying

Instructions:

1. Tofu cubes are fried in hot oil up to golden and crispy. Take out, then dry off with paper towels.
2. Grind the shallots, garlic, bird's eye chilies, shrimp paste, palm sugar, and tamarind paste into a paste in a mortar and pestle.
3. Heat a little oil in a different skillet, then sauté the paste up to aromatic.
4. Add salt and water. Let the Mixture to simmer and gradually thicken.
5. The fried tofu cubes Must be placed on a platter, then the sauce Must be poured over them.

136. Rendang Paru (Lung Rendang)

Prep Time: 20 mins
Cook Time: 2 hrs
Total Time: 2 hrs 20 mins
Servings: 4

Ingredients:

- 500g beef lungs (paru), cleaned and boiled up to tender, then slice into mini pieces
- 2 lemongrass stalks, bruised
- 3 kaffir lime leaves
- 1 turmeric leaf (non-compulsory), torn
- 1 cinnamon stick
- 2 star anise
- 3 cardamom pods
- 400ml coconut milk
- 1 tbsp tamarind paste
- 1 tbsp finely grated palm sugar or brown sugar
- Salt as needed
- Oil for cooking

Instructions:

1. Lemongrass, kaffir lime leaves, turmeric leaf, cinnamon stick, star anise, and cardamom pods are sautéed in hot oil up to fragrant.

2. Include the chop-up and cooked lung tissue. For a few mins, stir-fry.
3. Add the coconut milk, then boil the Mixture. Stirring occasionally, cook for about an hr over low heat.
4. Add salt, finely grated palm sugar, and tamarind paste. Cook the lung chunks and sauce further up to the latter are soft.
5. Serve rice or other traditional Indonesian side dishes with the rendang paru.

137.Kue Lumpur (Indonesian Mud Cake)

Prep Time: 15 mins
Cook Time: 30 mins
Total Time: 45 mins
Servings: 12 pieces

Ingredients:

- 1 cup of all-purpose flour
- 1 cup of sugar
- 1/2 cup of unsalted butter, dilute
- 3/4 cup of cocoa powder
- 1/2 cup of sweetened condensed milk
- 3 eggs
- 1 tsp vanilla extract
- 1/2 tsp baking powder
- Pinch of salt

Instructions:

1. Set the oven's temperature to 350°F (175°C). Prepare a muffin or cup ofcake pan with butter and flour.
2. Whisk the eggs, sugar, and vanilla extract in a combining bowl up to completely blended and just beginning to foam.
3. To the egg Mixture, add the dilute butter and sweetened condensed milk. Combine well.
4. Salt, baking soda, cocoa powder, and flour Must all be sifted in. Just combine by gently blending the dry components into the wet ones.
5. Fill every cup of in the muffin tin about two-thirds full with the batter.
6. Bake for about 25 to 30 mins in the preheated oven, or up to a toothpick inserted in the center comes out clean.
7. After removing the cakes from the oven, let them to cool in the pan for a short while before moving them to a wire rack to finish cooling.

Nutrition (per serving):

Cals: 220, Fat: 10g, Carbs: 32g

Protein: 4g

138. Tahu Gejrot Bandung (Bandung-style Fried Tofu)

Prep Time: 15 mins

Cook Time: 15 mins

Total Time: 30 mins

Servings: 4

Ingredients:

- 14 oz (400g) firm tofu, slice into cubes
- 1 cup of water
- 4 shallots, lightly split
- 2 red chilies, split
- 1 tsp tamarind paste
- 1 tsp palm sugar
- 1 tsp salt
- Oil, for frying

Instructions:

1. In a frying pan, heat the oil over medium-low heat. Tofu cubes Must be fried till golden and crispy. Drain and then pat dry with paper towels.
2. Water, tamarind paste, palm sugar, and salt Must all be combined in a pot. The sauce is made by bringing to a boil and then simmering for a short while.
3. Place the fried tofu cubes and red chilies on top in a serving dish.
4. Serve the tofu immediately after adding the tamarind sauce to it.

Nutrition (per serving):
Cals: 180, Fat: 10g

Carbs: 15g

Protein: 10g

139. Soto Banjar (Banjarese Beef Soup)

Prep Time: 20 mins

Cook Time: 2 hrs

Total Time: 2 hrs 20 mins

Servings: 6

Ingredients:

- 1 lb (450g) beef, slice into chunks
- 8 cups of beef broth
- 2 lemongrass stalks, bruised
- 4 kaffir lime leaves
- 2 cloves garlic, chop-up
- 1 onion, split
- 1 tsp turmeric powder
- 1 tsp coriander powder
- Salt and pepper as needed
- Rice noodles, cooked
- Bean sprouts, lime wedges, and fried shallots for garnish

Instructions:

1. Bring the beef broth to a boil in a pot. Cook the beef chunks up to cooked after adding them.
2. Garlic and onion Must be sautéed up to aromatic in a separate pan. Cook for one more min after adding the turmeric and coriander powder.
3. The beef broth Must be supplemented with the sautéed spices, lemongrass, kaffir lime leaves, salt, and pepper. To deepen the flavors, let it boil for approximately an hr or two.
4. Prepare cooked rice noodles for bowls.
5. Pour the soup over the beef chunks and noodles.
6. Bean sprouts, lime wedges, and fried shallots are used as garnish.

Nutrition (per serving):
Cals: 280, Fat: 8g

Carbs: 25g

Protein: 26g

140. Klepon Ketan Hitam Putih (Black and White Glutinous Rice Cake)

Prep Time: 30 mins

Cook Time: 30 mins

Total Time: 1 hr

Servings: 16 pieces

Ingredients:

- 1 cup of black glutinous rice flour
- 1 cup of white glutinous rice flour
- 3/4 cup of palm sugar, finely grated
- 1/2 cup of finely grated coconut
- A pinch of salt
- Water
- Banana leaves, slice into 4x4 inch squares

Instructions:

1. The black glutinous rice flour Must be combined with a little water in separate bowls to create a dough-like consistency. Use the white glutinous rice flour in the same manner.
2. A mini amount of the dark dough Must be flattened in your hand. Wrap the dough around a mini bit of palm sugar that has been placed in the center. Form a little ball out of it. Continue by using the white dough.
3. Put some water on to boil. Rice balls Must be dropped into boiling water and cooked up to they float to the top. Let them drain after removing with a slotted spoon.
4. Grate some coconut and roll the cooked rice balls in it.
5. Every rice cake Must be served on a piece of banana leaf.

Nutrition (per serving):

Cals: 120, Fat: 2g

Carbs: 26g

Protein: 1g

141. Sambal Tumpang (East Javanese Chili Sauce)

Prep Time: 15 mins

Cook Time: 15 mins

Total Time: 30 mins

Servings: 6

Ingredients:

- 10 red bird's eye chilies, chop-up
- 5 cloves garlic
- 2 shallots
- 1 tsp shrimp paste
- 1 tsp palm sugar
- 1 tsp salt
- 1 tbsp oil

Instructions:

1. To make a paste, combine the red chilies, garlic, shallots, and shrimp paste.
2. Over medium heat, warm the oil in the pan.
3. Add the chili paste and cook up to fragrant for a few mins.
4. After adding salt and palm sugar, simmer for a few more mins.
5. Before serving, take out from the heat and let it cool.

142. Bubur Ketan Putih (White Glutinous Rice Porridge)

Prep Time: 4 hrs (includes soaking time)

Cook Time: 1 hr

Total Time: 5 hrs

Servings: 4

Ingredients:

- 1 cup of glutinous rice, soaked for 4 hrs and drained
- 4 cups of coconut milk
- 1/2 cup of sugar
- 1/2 tsp salt
- Banana slices and toasted coconut for garnish

Instructions:

1. The sticky rice, coconut milk, sugar, and salt Must all be combined in a pot.
2. Stirring constantly to prevent sticking, simmer the Mixture over medium-low heat for about an hr, or up to the rice is cooked and the porridge has thickened.

3. Hot porridge Must be served with toasted coconut and banana slices as garnish.

143. Papeda Kuah Udang (Sago Porridge with Shrimp Soup)

Prep Time: 10 mins

Cook Time: 30 mins

Total Time: 40 mins

Servings: 4

Ingredients:

- 1 cup of sago pearls
- 4 cups of water
- 200g shrimp, peel off and deveined
- 2 cloves garlic, chop-up
- 1 tsp turmeric powder
- Salt as needed
- Chop-up scallions and fried shallots for garnish

Instructions:

1. Bring the water to a boil in a pot. Sago pearls are added, cooked while stirring occasionally up to they become translucent. Drain, then set apart.
2. Sauté the turmeric powder and chop-up garlic up to fragrant in a separate pot.
3. When the shrimp are pink, add them and continue to boil.
4. Add the water, then simmer the Mixture. As needed, add salt.
5. Sago pearls that have been cooked Must be placed in a bowl, then the shrimp soup Must be poured over them. Add fried shallots and split scallions as a garnish.

144. Rendang Limpa (Spleen Rendang)

Prep Time: 20 mins

Cook Time: 2 hrs

Total Time: 2 hrs 20 mins

Servings: 4

Ingredients:

- 500g spleen, split into thin pieces
- 2 lemongrass stalks, bruised
- 4 kaffir lime leaves
- 400ml coconut milk
- 2 tbsp oil
- Salt as needed

Instructions:

1. Split spleen is cooked in hot oil up to it begins to turn somewhat brown.
2. Coconut milk, kaffir lime leaves, and lemongrass Must all be added to the pan. Stir thoroughly.
3. For approximately two hrs, or up to the spleen is

soft and the sauce has thickened, simmer the Mixture, covered, over low heat.

4. As needed, add salt to the dish.
5. Steamed rice Must be served with the limp rendang.

145. Kue Ape (Indonesian Pancake with Banana)

Prep Time: 15 mins

Cook Time: 20 mins

Total Time: 35 mins

Servings: 4

Ingredients:

- 2 ripe bananas, mashed
- 1 cup of all-purpose flour
- 1/2 cup of coconut milk
- 1/4 cup of sugar
- 1/4 tsp salt
- 1/2 tsp vanilla extract
- 1/4 tsp baking powder
- Oil for frying

Instructions:

1. The mashed bananas, flour, coconut milk, sugar, salt, vanilla extract, and baking powder Must all be combined in a combining bowl. Combine thoroughly up to a smooth batter is achieved.
2. Add a little oil to a non-stick pan that is already heated over medium heat.
3. To make a pancake, spoon some batter onto the pan. Cook up to surface bubbles appear, then turn and continue to cook the other side up to golden.
4. With the remaining batter, repeat the procedure.
5. Warm Indonesian pancakes, or "Kue Ape," are served.

Nutrition (per serving):

Cals: 220, Carbs: 45g

Protein: 3g, Fat: 4g, Fiber: 2g

146. Sate Kerbau (Buffalo Satay)

Prep Time: 30 mins

Cook Time: 15 mins

Total Time: 45 mins

Servings: 6

Ingredients:

- 1 lb buffalo meat, slice into thin strips
- 1 tbsp vegetable oil
- 2 cloves garlic, chop-up
- 1 tsp ground coriander
- 1 tsp ground turmeric
- 1 tsp cumin

- 1 tsp brown sugar
- Salt and pepper as needed
- Bamboo skewers, soaked in water

Instructions:

1. The vegetable oil, chop-up garlic, ground cumin, ground turmeric, ground coriander, and salt and pepper Must all be combined in a bowl. To make a marinade, thoroughly combine.
2. Then add the buffalo meat and evenly coat it with the marinade. Give it at least an hr to marinate.
3. Onto the bamboo skewers that have been soaked, thread the marinated buffalo meat.
4. A grill or grill pan Must be preheated to high heat. The buffalo satay skewers Must be cooked through and slightly browned after grilling them for 5 to 7 mins on every side.
5. The Sate Kerbau Must be served hot with rice and peanut sauce.

Nutrition (per serving):

Cals: 220, Carbs: 3g

Protein: 25g, Fat: 12g, Fiber: 1g

147. Soto Medan (Medan-style Chicken Soup)

Prep Time: 20 mins

Cook Time: 1 hr

Total Time: 1 hr 20 mins

Servings: 4

Ingredients:

- 1 whole chicken, slice into parts
- 8 cups of water
- 2 lemongrass stalks, bruised
- 3 kaffir lime leaves
- 1 inch ginger, split
- 2 cloves garlic, chop-up
- 1 tsp ground turmeric
- Salt and pepper as needed
- Rice vermicelli, cooked
- Bean sprouts
- Fried shallots
- Hard-boiled eggs, halved
- Lime wedges
- Fresh cilantro, chop-up

Instructions:

1. Bring the water in a pot to a boil before adding the chicken parts. Cook the chicken up to it is thoroughly done and tender. Shred the chicken after removing it from the soup.
2. Add the skin and bones back to the broth. Add ground turmeric, ginger, garlic, kaffir lime leaves,

and lemongrass. Simmer to bring out the flavors for about 30 to 40 mins.

3. Salt and pepper the broth after straining the sediments out.
4. Cooked rice vermicelli, diced chicken, bean sprouts, and fried shallots Must all be combined in a bowl before serving. Over the ingredients, pour the hot broth.
5. Hard-boiled eggs slice in half, lime wedges, and chop-up cilantro can be used as garnish.
6. Hot Soto Medan Must be served.

Nutrition (per serving):
Cals: 350, Carbs: 20g

Protein: 30g, Fat: 16g, Fiber: 3g

148. Tahu Gimbal (Gimbal Tofu)

Prep Time: 20 mins

Cook Time: 10 mins

Total Time: 30 mins

Servings: 4

Ingredients:
- 1 block firm tofu, slice into cubes
- 1 cup of bean sprouts
- 1 cucumber, julienned
- 1 mini carrot, julienned
- 1 cup of cabbage, thinly split
- 1/2 cup of fried shallots
- 1/2 cup of peanuts, roasted and crushed
- 1/4 cup of sweet soy sauce (kecap manis)
- 2 tbsp tamarind pulp, soaked in water and strained
- 2 cloves garlic, chop-up
- 2 red chilies, chop-up
- Salt and sugar as needed
- Cooking oil for frying

Instructions:
1. Tofu cubes Must be fried in hot frying oil up to crisp and golden brown. Take out, then dry off with paper towels.
2. To make the sauce, combine the tamarind juice, chop-up garlic, chop-up chiles, salt, and sugar in a bowl.
3. Place the split cabbage, bean sprouts, cucumber, carrot, and fried tofu on a serving platter.
4. Pour the tamarind sauce and sweet soy sauce over the ingredients.
5. Add fried shallots and cut up, roasted peanuts.
6. Serve the Tahu Gimbal with rice or as a light salad.

Nutrition (per serving):
Cals: 280, Carbs: 20g

Protein: 14g, Fat: 18g

Fiber: 5g

149. Kue Serabi Solo (Solo-style Coconut Pancakes)

Prep Time: 15 mins

Cook Time: 20 mins

Total Time: 35 mins

Servings: Makes about 10-12 pancakes

Ingredients:
- 1 cup of rice flour
- 1/2 cup of coconut milk
- 1/4 cup of granulated sugar
- 1/4 tsp salt
- 1/4 tsp vanilla extract
- 1/2 cup of water
- Finely grated coconut for topping

Instructions:
1. Rice flour, coconut milk, sugar, salt, and vanilla essence Must all be combined in a bowl.
2. Water Must be added gradually while combining to create a smooth batter.
3. A nonstick skillet Must be heated to medium.
4. To make a pancake, pour a ladleful of the batter onto the griddle.
5. Sprinkle some finely grated coconut on top after cooking up to mini holes start to emerge on the surface.
6. Cook the pancake for one more min, or up to it is thoroughly cooked and the edges are just beginning to crisp.
7. With the remaining batter, repeat the procedure.
8. Warm coconut pancakes Must be served.

NUTRITION INFO (per serving):
Cals: 120 kcal, Carbs: 23 g

Protein: 2 g, Fat: 2 g, Fiber: 1 g

150. Sate Udang (Shrimp Satay)

Prep Time: 30 mins

Cook Time: 10 mins

Total Time: 40 mins

Servings: Makes about 16-20 skewers

Ingredients:
- 1 lb Big shrimp, peel off and deveined
- 2 tbsp soy sauce
- 2 tbsp vegetable oil
- 2 cloves garlic, chop-up
- 1 tsp turmeric powder
- 1 tsp cumin powder
- 1 tsp coriander powder

- 1 tbsp brown sugar
- Bamboo skewers, soaked in water

Instructions:

1. To make the marinade, combine the soy sauce, vegetable oil, chop-up garlic, turmeric, cumin, coriander, and brown sugar in a bowl.
2. Add the shrimp and thoroughly coat them in the marinade. For 15 to 20 mins, let them marinade.
3. To the bamboo skewers that have been soaked, thread the marinated shrimp.
4. A grill or grill pan Must be preheated to high heat.
5. The shrimp skewers Must be cooked through and slightly browned after grilling them for two to three mins on every side.
6. Serve the shrimp satay with your favorite dipping sauce, such as peanut sauce.

NUTRITION INFO (per serving, without sauce):
Cals: 70 kcal, Carbs: 2 g

Protein: 10 g, Fat: 2 g, Fiber: 0 g

151. Sambal Tempoyak (Fermented Durian Chili Sauce)

Prep Time: 15 mins

Cook Time: 20 mins

Total Time: 35 mins

Servings: 4

Ingredients:

- 200g tempoyak (fermented durian), mashed
- 10 red chili peppers, chop-up
- 5 shallots, chop-up
- 3 cloves garlic, chop-up
- 1 tsp shrimp paste (belacan)
- 1 tbsp tamarind paste
- 1 tsp sugar
- Salt as needed
- Oil for frying

Instructions:

1. Shallots and garlic are sautéed in hot oil up to aromatic.
2. Add the shrimp paste and diced chile peppers. Peppers Must be melted in the sauté.
3. Add tamarind paste, sugar, salt, and mashed tempeh. Combine thoroughly and heat for a short while.
4. If necessary, taste and adjust the seasoning.
5. Before serving, take out from the heat and let it cool.
6. Serve the tempoyak sambal with rice or as a side dish.

NUTRITION INFO:
Cals: 120 kcal, Protein: 2g
Fat: 8g, Carbs: 10g, Fiber: 2g

152. Tumis Jamur Tiram (Stir-fried Oyster Mushrooms)

Prep Time: 10 mins

Cook Time: 15 mins

Total Time: 25 mins

Servings: 3

Ingredients:

- 300g oyster mushrooms, cleaned and split
- 1 onion, thinly split
- 2 cloves garlic, chop-up
- 1 red chili pepper, split
- 1 green chili pepper, split
- 1 tbsp oyster sauce
- 1 tbsp soy sauce
- 1 tsp sugar
- Salt and pepper as needed
- Oil for cooking

Instructions:

1. In a pan or wok, heat the oil over medium-high heat.
2. Add chop-up onion and chop-up garlic. Sauté the onion up to it turns translucent.
3. Add the chile peppers and the slice mushrooms. The mushrooms Must be stir-fried for a few mins to become soft.
4. Add sugar, salt, pepper, oyster sauce, and soy sauce. For another 2 to 3 mins, stir-fry.
5. If necessary, taste and adjust the seasoning.
6. Serve the stir-fried oyster mushrooms with steamed rice after removing from the heat.

NUTRITION INFO:
Cals: 80 kcal, Protein: 4g, Fat: 2g

Carbs: 12g, Fiber: 3g

153. Papeda Kuah Tenggiri (Sago Porridge with Spanish Mackerel Soup)

Prep Time: 20 mins

Cook Time: 40 mins

Total Time: 1 hr

Servings: 6

Ingredients:

- 200g sago pearls
- 300g Spanish mackerel fillets, slice into chunks
- 1 lemongrass stalk, smashed
- 2 kaffir lime leaves
- 3 cloves garlic, chop-up

- 1 onion, chop-up
- 2 red chili peppers, split
- 1 tbsp cooking oil
- 1 liter fish or vegetable broth
- Salt as needed

Instructions:

1. Sago pearls Must be rinsed in cold water and laid aside.
2. Oil in a pot is heated to medium heat. Garlic and onion are sautéed till aromatic.
3. For a few mins, add the chunks of Spanish mackerel and sauté.
4. Lemongrass, kaffir lime leaves, and chili peppers are added after pouring in the broth. Simmer for a while.
5. Sago pearls Must be added, with sporadic stirring to prevent sticking. Sago pearls are cooked till they become translucent.
6. Eliminate the kaffir lime and lemongrass leaves. As needed, add salt to the soup.
7. Serve the hot papeda kuah tenggiri as a hearty soup or porridge dish.

NUTRITION INFO:

Cals: 250 kcal, Protein: 15g

Fat: 10g, Carbs: 25g, Fiber: 1g

154. Rendang Lidah (Tongue Rendang)

Prep Time: 20 mins

Cook Time: 3 hrs

Total Time: 3 hrs 20 mins

Servings: 4

Ingredients:

- 500g beef tongue, cleaned and split
- 2 onions, chop-up
- 3 cloves garlic, chop-up
- 2 lemongrass stalks, bruised
- 4 kaffir lime leaves
- 2 tbsp rendang spice paste (available in stores or homemade)
- 400ml coconut milk
- 1 tbsp tamarind paste
- 1 tsp sugar
- Salt as needed
- Cooking oil

Instructions:

1. The chop-up onions and chop-up garlic Must be sautéed in hot oil up to aromatic.
2. Cook the rendang spice paste up to aromatic after adding.
3. Split beef tongue Must be added and cooked up to the outside is no longer pink.

4. Lemongrass, kaffir lime leaves, tamarind paste, sugar, and salt are added after pouring in the coconut milk.
5. After bringing to a boil, turn down the heat. Stirring regularly, simmer the beef tongue for about 2.5 to 3 hrs, or up to it is soft and the sauce has thickened.
6. If necessary, adjust the seasoning. Rich, complex flavor Must be included in the rendang.
7. Serve steamed rice beside the rendang lidah.

NUTRITION INFO:

Cals: 380 kcal, Protein: 18g

Fat: 30g, Carbs: 10g, Fiber: 1g

155. Soto Bandung (Bandung-style Chicken Soup)

Prep Time: 20 mins

Cook Time: 1 hr

Total Time: 1 hr 20 mins

Servings: 4

Ingredients:

- 500g chicken, slice into pieces
- 1 liter water
- 2 lemongrass stalks, bruised
- 3 kaffir lime leaves
- 2 bay leaves
- 3 cloves garlic, chop-up
- 1 tsp turmeric powder
- 1 tsp ground coriander
- Salt and pepper as needed
- 100g glass noodles, soaked in hot water and drained
- 100g bean sprouts
- 2 hard-boiled eggs, halved
- Fried shallots for garnish
- Fresh cilantro leaves for garnish
- Lime wedges for serving

Instructions:

1. Bring water to a boil in a pot, then add the chicken pieces. Cook the chicken up to it is tender. Shred the chicken after removing it from the soup. Place aside.
2. Lemongrass, kaffir lime leaves, bay leaves, garlic, turmeric powder, ground coriander, salt, and pepper Must all be added to the same pot. For 20 mins, simmer.
3. Return the broth to the pot after straining the solids out.
4. Glass noodles, shredded chicken, and bean sprouts Must be put in serving dishes before serving. Over them, pour the hot broth.

5. Add fried shallots, hard-boiled eggs, and cilantro leaves as garnish.
6. If desired, serve with lime wedges and sambal.

NUTRITION INFO:

Cals: ~250 per serving

Protein: ~20g, Carbs: ~20g

Fat: ~10g

156. Nasi Krawu (East Javanese Rice Dish)

Prep Time: 30 mins

Cook Time: 1 hr

Total Time: 1 hr 30 mins

Servings: 6

Ingredients:

- 2 cups of rice, cooked
- 200g beef, thinly split and grilled
- 200g roasted shredded coconut
- 100g fried shallots
- 6 boiled eggs, peel off
- 200g empal gepuk (sweet and spicy fried beef)
- Sambal kecap (sweet soy sauce chili sauce)
- Banana leaves for serving

Instructions:

1. A bit of rice Must be placed on a piece of banana leaf.
2. On top of the rice, place split grilled meat, roasted shredded coconut, fried shallots, boiled eggs, and empal gepuk.
3. To create a tidy box/pkg, wrap the rice and contents in the banana leaf.
4. Sambal kecap Must be served on the side.

NUTRITION INFO:

Cals: ~450 per serving, Protein: ~20g

Carbs: ~40g, Fat: ~25g

157. Sambal Roa (Smoked Fish Chili Sauce)

Prep Time: 15 mins

Cook Time: 15 mins

Total Time: 30 mins

Servings: Makes about 1 cup of

Ingredients:

- 100g smoked fish (such as mackerel), flaked
- 10 red chili peppers, deseeded and split
- 5 shallots, split
- 3 cloves garlic
- 1 tomato, chop-up
- 1 tsp shrimp paste (terasi), toasted
- 1 tsp palm sugar
- Salt as needed
- Lime juice as needed

Instructions:

1. The shrimp paste Must be dry-roasted up to aromatic in a pan.
2. Grind the roasted shrimp paste, split chili peppers, shallots, and garlic into a paste in a mortar and pestle.
3. The paste Must be sautéed in a mini amount of hot oil up to aromatic.
4. Add salt, palm sugar, tomato diced, flakes smoked fish, and tomato. Cook the Mixture up to it thickens.
5. If necessary, season with more salt and lime juice.
6. The sambal Must cool before being served.

NUTRITION INFO:

Cals: ~30 per tbsp

Protein: ~2g, Carbs: ~3g

Fat: ~1g

158. Tumis Kacang Panjang (Stir-fried Yardlong Beans)

Prep Time: 10 mins

Cook Time: 10 mins

Total Time: 20 mins

Servings: 4

Ingredients:

- 300g yardlong beans (snake beans), slice into 2-inch pieces
- 2 cloves garlic, chop-up
- 1 red chili pepper, split
- 1 tsp shrimp paste (terasi)
- 1 tsp palm sugar
- 1 tbsp soy sauce
- Salt as needed
- Oil for cooking

Instructions:

1. Oil in a pan is heated to medium heat.
2. Split chile pepper and chop-up garlic are sautéed up to aromatic.
3. Stir-fry the shrimp paste for a min to thoroughly incorporate it in.
4. When the yardlong beans are tender-crisp, add them to the stir-fry and stir-fry for an additional 5-7 mins.
5. Add salt, soy sauce, and palm sugar for flavoring. To blend, stir.
6. If necessary, taste and adjust the seasoning.
7. Serve as a side dish after being taken off the heat.

NUTRITION INFO:

Cals: ~60 per serving

Protein: ~2g, Carbs: ~8g

Fat: ~2g

159. Soto Lamongan (Lamongan-style Chicken Soup)

Prep Time: 20 mins

Cook Time: 1 hr

Total Time: 1 hr 20 mins

Servings: 4

Ingredients:

- 500g chicken pieces (preferably bone-in)
- 2 stalks lemongrass, bruised
- 3 kaffir lime leaves
- 3 cloves garlic, chop-up
- 1 onion, chop-up
- 1 tsp turmeric powder
- 1 tsp ground coriander
- 1/2 tsp ground cumin
- Salt and pepper as needed
- 8 cups of chicken broth
- Rice vermicelli, cooked
- Hard-boiled eggs, halved
- Fried shallots for garnish
- Chop-up green onions for garnish
- Lime wedges

Instructions:

1. Garlic and onion Must be sautéed in a pot up to aromatic.
2. Salt, pepper, coriander, cumin, and turmeric Must be added. For one min, cook.
3. Cook till browned after adding the chicken pieces.
4. Chicken broth Must be added, along with lemongrass and kaffir lime leaves. When chicken is tender, simmer.
5. Chicken Must be taken out of the soup, shredded, and kept aside.
6. Filter the broth to get rid of any solids.
7. When ready to serve, put cooked rice vermicelli and shredded chicken in bowls and top with hot broth.
8. Add fried shallots, lime wedges, chop-up green onions, and hard-boiled eggs as garnish.

Nutrition (per serving - approximate):

Cals: 300, Protein: 25g

Carbs: 20g

Fat: 12g

160. Lontong Solo (Solo-style Rice Cake)

Prep Time: 30 mins

Cook Time: 2 hrs

Total Time: 2 hrs 30 mins

Servings: 6

Ingredients:

- 2 cups of rice, soaked for 2 hrs and drained
- Banana leaves, slice into rectangles and blanched
- 1 tsp salt
- Water

Instructions:

1. Rice Must be soaked before grinding it into a coarse paste.
2. To make a thick batter, combine salt and a little extra water.
3. A scoop of the rice batter Must be placed in the center of a cross formed by two pieces of blanched banana leaves.
4. The banana leaves Must be tightly rolled up.
5. Use toothpicks or twine to tie the box/pkg closed.
6. To cook and firm the rice cakes, steam the packets for 1.5 to 2 hrs.
7. After the rice cake has cooled, slice it open.

Nutrition (per serving - approximate):

Cals: 180, Protein: 3g

Carbs: 40g, Fat: 0g

161. Kue Lumpur Bandung (Bandung-style Mud Cake)

Prep Time: 15 mins

Cook Time: 30 mins

Total Time: 45 mins

Servings: 8

Ingredients:

- 1 cup of all-purpose flour
- 1/2 cup of cocoa powder
- 1/2 tsp baking powder
- 1/4 tsp salt
- 3/4 cup of sugar
- 2 eggs
- 1/2 cup of milk
- 1/4 cup of dilute butter
- 1 tsp vanilla extract

Instructions:

1. Prepare a muffin pan or tiny cake molds with greasing and preheat the oven to 350°F (175°C).
2. Combine the flour, baking soda, salt, and cocoa powder in a bowl.
3. Beat sugar and eggs up to they are light and frothy in a another bowl.
4. While combining, gradually include the milk, dilute butter, and vanilla extract.

5. Fold the dry ingredients in gradually up to barely incorporated.
6. The batter Must be poured into every prepared mold up to it is about 3/4 filled.
7. If using a toothpick, bake for about 25 to 30 mins, or up to it comes out clean.
8. Before removing the cakes from the molds, let them cool.

Nutrition (per serving - approximate):
Cals: 220, Protein: 4g, Carbs: 35g

Fat: 8g

162. Sate Kuda (Horse Satay)

Prep Time: 1 hr

Cook Time: 15 mins

Total Time: 1 hr 15 mins

Servings: 4

Ingredients:
- 500g horse meat, slice into mini cubes
- 1 onion, finely grated
- 3 cloves garlic, chop-up
- 1 tsp ground turmeric
- 1 tsp ground coriander
- 1 tsp ground cumin
- 1/2 tsp chili powder (adjust as needed)
- 2 tbsp soy sauce
- 1 tbsp vegetable oil
- Bamboo skewers, soaked in water

Instructions:
1. To make a marinade, combine the finely grated onion, chop-up garlic, turmeric, coriander, cumin, chili powder, soy sauce, and vegetable oil in a bowl.
2. Making sure that every piece is coated, add the cubes of horse meat to the marinade. For at least 30 mins, marinate.
3. Place the marinated horse meat on bamboo skewers that have been soaked.
4. The skewers Must be grilled or broiled for 10 to 15 mins, turning them once or twice, or up to the meat is cooked through and slightly browned.
5. If desired, serve with rice and peanut sauce.

Nutrition (per serving - approximate):
Cals: 220, Protein: 25g

Carbs: 4g, Fat: 12g

Prep Time: 20 mins

Cook Time: 2 hrs

Total Time: 2 hrs 20 mins

Servings: 4

Ingredients:
- 500g beef, slice into chunks
- 2 potatoes, peel off and cubed
- 2 tomatoes, quartered
- 2 lemongrass stalks, bruised
- 4 kaffir lime leaves
- 2 bay leaves
- 1 cinnamon stick
- 4 cloves
- 1 tsp turmeric powder
- 1 tsp coriander powder
- Salt and pepper as needed
- 1 tbsp oil for cooking
- 1 onion, lightly chop-up
- 3 cloves garlic, chop-up
- 1 tsp ginger, chop-up
- 1 tsp galangal, chop-up
- 4 cups of beef broth
- 1 cup of coconut milk
- Fried shallots and chop-up cilantro for garnish
- Sambal (chili sauce) for serving

Instructions:
1. The chop-up onion, garlic, ginger, and galangal Must be sautéed in hot oil up to aromatic.
2. Cook the beef after adding it up to the color changes. Salt, pepper, turmeric, and coriander powder Must be added. Stir thoroughly.
3. Pour the coconut milk and beef broth in. Add bay leaves, cinnamon sticks, cloves, lemongrass, and kaffir lime leaves.
4. After bringing the soup to a boil, turn down the heat. For about two hrs, with the lid on, cook the beef up to it is soft.
5. Once the potatoes and tomatoes are added, boil the Mixture for a further few mins.
6. seasoning as necessary. Eliminate the cloves, cinnamon stick, and bay leaves.
7. Hot soup Must be served with chop-up cilantro and fried shallots as garnish. Sambal Must be served on the side.

163. Soto Betawi Makasar (Makasar-style Beef Soup)

164. Sambal Dabu-Dabu (Manado-style Chili Sauce)

Prep Time: 15 mins

Cook Time: 0 mins

Total Time: 15 mins

Servings: Makes about 1 cup of

Ingredients:

- 5-6 bird's eye chilies, lightly chop-up
- 2 tomatoes, lightly chop-up
- 1 mini red onion, lightly chop-up
- 2 cloves garlic, chop-up
- 2 tbsp lime juice
- 1 tbsp fish sauce
- Salt and sugar as needed

Instructions:

1. Combine the chop-up tomatoes, onions, garlic, and chilies in a bowl.
2. Add fish sauce, sugar, salt, and lime juice. Depending on your preference for spice, saltiness, and acidity, adjust the seasoning.
3. Before serving, thoroughly combine everything and set it aside for a while.

165. Papeda Kuah Cumi (Sago Porridge with Squid Soup)

Prep Time: 20 mins

Cook Time: 1 hr

Total Time: 1 hr 20 mins

Servings: 4

Ingredients:

- 200g squid, cleaned and split
- 1 cup of sago pearls
- 4 cups of water
- 2 cloves garlic, chop-up
- 1 onion, chop-up
- 2 tomatoes, chop-up
- 2 lemongrass stalks, bruised
- 2 kaffir lime leaves
- Salt and pepper as needed

Instructions:

1. Bring the water to a boil in a pot. Sago pearls Must be added and cooked up to transparent. Drain, then set apart.
2. Sauté the chop-up garlic and lightly diced onion up to aromatic in a separate pot.
3. Squid slices Must be added and cooked up to opaque.
4. Tomatoes, lemongrass, and kaffir lime leaves Must all be included. Cook the tomatoes for a little while up to they are tender.
5. Add water and the cooked sago pearls. Simmer the soup for 30 to 40 mins.
6. As desired, season the soup with salt and pepper.

7. Papeda Kuah Cumi Must be served hot.

Nutrition (per serving):

Cals: 220 kcal, Protein: 10g

Carbs: 45g, Fat: 1g, Fiber: 3g

166. Rendang Babat (Tripe Rendang)

Prep Time: 30 mins

Cook Time: 3 hrs

Total Time: 3 hrs 30 mins

Servings: 6

Ingredients:

- 500g tripe, cleaned and slice into bite-sized pieces
- 2 cups of coconut milk
- 2 lemongrass stalks, bruised
- 3 kaffir lime leaves
- 2 turmeric leaves (or 1/2 tsp turmeric powder)
- 1 cinnamon stick
- 3 cardamom pods
- 3 cloves
- 1 star anise
- 1 cup of water
- Salt and sugar as needed

Instructions:

1. Tripe, coconut milk, lemongrass, kaffir lime leaves, turmeric powder or leaves, cinnamon stick, cardamom pods, cloves, and star anise Must all be combined in a pot.
2. Bring the Mixture to a boil after adding water. Once the tripe is soft and the flavors are well-balanced, turn the heat down to low and let it simmer for about two to three hrs.
3. Stir and check the liquid level every now and then. When necessary, add extra water.
4. Add salt and sugar as needed once the tripe is soft and the sauce has thickened. Cooking time Must be extended by 15 to 20 mins.
5. Serve steamed rice alongside the Rendang Babat.

Nutrition (per serving):

Cals: 380 kcal, Protein: 18g

Carbs: 10g

Fat: 30g, Fiber: 2g

167. Rendang Paru (Lung Rendang)

Prep Time: 15 mins

Cook Time: 2 hrs

Total Time: 2 hrs 15 mins

Servings: 4

Ingredients:

- 500 grams lung (paru), cleaned and slice into bite-sized pieces

- 2 shallots, lightly chop-up
- 3 cloves garlic, chop-up
- 2 lemongrass stalks, bruised
- 2 kaffir lime leaves
- 1 turmeric leaf (non-compulsory)
- 1 cinnamon stick
- 2 cardamom pods
- 2 cloves
- 1 tsp ground coriander
- 1 tsp ground cumin
- 1 tsp tamarind paste
- 400 ml coconut milk
- 200 ml water
- 2 tbsp oil
- Salt and sugar as needed

Instructions:

1. Oil in a pot is heated to medium heat. When aromatic, add the shallots and garlic.
2. Sauté the lung pieces up to they turn color.
3. Add the ground cloves, cardamom pods, cinnamon stick, ground cumin, and ground coriander. Combine thoroughly.
4. Add water and coconut milk. Add the tamarind paste, salt, sugar, kaffir lime leaves, turmeric leaf (if using), and lemongrass.
5. Stir and heat to simmering. Cooking the lung on low heat with the lid on takes about two hrs, or up to the lung is soft and the sauce has thickened.
6. To prevent sticking and burning, stir occasionally. If necessary, adjust the seasoning.
7. Take out from heat when the sauce has thickened and the lung is soft.
8. Serve steamed rice beside the rendang paru.

168. Kue Ape (Indonesian Pancake with Banana)

Prep Time: 10 mins
Cook Time: 20 mins
Total Time: 30 mins
Servings: 6

Ingredients:

- 2 ripe bananas, mashed
- 1 cup of all-purpose flour
- 1/2 cup of rice flour
- 1/2 cup of coconut milk
- 1/2 cup of water
- 1/4 cup of granulated sugar
- 1/2 tsp salt
- 1/2 tsp vanilla extract
- 1/4 tsp baking powder
- Oil for frying

Instructions:

1. The following ingredients Must be thoroughly blended in a bowl: mashed bananas, all-purpose flour, rice flour, coconut milk, water, granulated sugar, salt, vanilla extract, and baking powder.
2. Lightly oil and heat a kue ape mold or mini pancake pan.
3. Mini amounts of the batter Must be poured into every mold cavity.
4. Cook the bottom up to it turns golden brown before flipping it over to cook the other side.
5. Till all of the batter is consumed, repeat the process.
6. Kue ape Must be served hot.

169. Sate Kerbau (Buffalo Satay)

Prep Time: 30 mins
Cook Time: 15 mins
Total Time: 45 mins
Servings: 4

Ingredients:

- 500 grams buffalo meat, slice into mini cubes
- 1 lemongrass stalk, lightly chop-up
- 2 cloves garlic, chop-up
- 1 tsp turmeric powder
- 1 tsp coriander powder
- 1 tsp cumin powder
- 1 tbsp soy sauce
- 1 tbsp vegetable oil
- Bamboo skewers, soaked in water

Instructions:

1. To make the marinade, combine the lemongrass, garlic, turmeric, coriander, and cumin powders with the soy sauce and vegetable oil in a bowl.
2. Add the cubes of buffalo meat to the marinade and thoroughly coat them. For at least 20 mins, marinate.
3. The soaking bamboo skewers are then threaded with the marinated meat.
4. The meat Must be cooked through and slightly browned after grilling or cooking the skewers for around 10-15 mins on a hot grill or stovetop grill pan.
5. Rice and peanut sauce Must be served with the sate kerbau.

170. Soto Medan (Medan-style Chicken Soup)

Prep Time: 20 mins
Cook Time: 1 hr
Total Time: 1 hr 20 mins
Servings: 6

Ingredients:

- 1 whole chicken, slice into parts
- 2 lemongrass stalks, bruised
- 3 kaffir lime leaves
- 2 bay leaves
- 4 cloves garlic, chop-up
- 2 shallots, lightly chop-up
- 1 tsp ground turmeric
- 1 tsp ground coriander
- 1 tsp ground cumin
- 1 tsp ground ginger
- 1 tsp ground white pepper
- Salt as needed
- Rice vermicelli, cooked
- Bean sprouts
- Fried shallots
- Hard-boiled eggs, halved
- Lime wedges
- Chop-up green onions and cilantro for garnish

Instructions:

1. The chicken Must be cooked and soft after being boiled in a saucepan with enough water to cover the chicken. Whenever foam appears on the surface, skim it off.
2. Shred the chicken after removing it from the soup. Place aside.
3. Garlic and shallots Must be sautéed up to aromatic in a separate saucepan.
4. Salt, ground white pepper, ground ginger, ground coriander, ground cumin, and ground turmeric Must be added. Combine thoroughly.
5. Stir in the shredded chicken to evenly distribute the spices.
6. Add the chicken stock you made while boiling the chicken.
7. Add bay leaves, lemongrass, and kaffir lime leaves. Let the soup boil for 30 to 40 mins to let the flavors meld.
8. If necessary, adjust the seasoning.
9. Bean sprouts and cooked rice vermicelli Must be placed in bowls for serving. Over the noodles, ladle the heated soup.
10. Add cilantro, lime wedges, chop-up green onions, hard-boiled eggs in halves, and fried shallots on top.
11. Hot soto Medan Must be served.

171.Kue Cucur Solo (Solo-style Fried Pancake with Palm Sugar)

Prep Time: 15 mins
Cook Time: 20 mins
Total Time: 35 mins
Servings: 4

Ingredients:

- 1 cup of rice flour
- 1/4 cup of all-purpose flour
- 1/2 tsp baking powder
- 1/2 tsp salt
- 1 cup of coconut milk
- 1/2 cup of water
- 1/2 cup of palm sugar, finely grated or chop-up
- Oil for frying

Instructions:

1. Rice flour, all-purpose flour, baking soda, and salt Must be combined in a combining dish.
2. Stirring will help you add the water and coconut milk gradually to create a smooth batter.
3. Oil in a pan is heated to medium heat.
4. A tiny amount of batter Must be scooped with a spoon, gently dropped into the hot oil, and formed into a circle. Cook in groups.
5. Fry up to both sides are crispy and golden. Eliminate and absorb extra oil on paper towels.
6. Sprinkle finely grated or chop-up palm sugar on top of every pancake while it is still warm.
7. Kue Cucur Solo Must be served warm.

Nutrition (per serving):
Cals: 250, Fat: 6g

Carbs: 45g

Protein: 3g

172. Sate Kerbau Batak (Batak-style Buffalo Satay)

Prep Time: 30 mins
Cook Time: 15 mins
Total Time: 45 mins
Servings: 6

Ingredients:

- 1 lb buffalo meat, slice into thin strips
- 2 shallots, lightly chop-up
- 3 cloves garlic, chop-up
- 1 tsp ginger paste
- 1 tsp turmeric powder
- 1 tsp lemongrass paste
- 2 tbsp vegetable oil
- Salt and pepper as needed
- Bamboo skewers, soaked in water

Instructions:

1. Shallots, garlic, ginger, turmeric, and lemongrass paste are combined with vegetable oil, salt, and pepper in a bowl to produce a marinade.
2. Strips of buffalo meat Must be thoroughly coated in the marinade. Give the meat at least 20 mins to marinade.
3. The soaking bamboo skewers are then threaded with the marinated meat.
4. Grill or broil the skewers for 6 to 8 mins on every side, or up to the meat is done.
5. Sate Kerbau Batak Must be served hot with rice and your choice of dipping sauce.

Nutrition (per serving):
Cals: 280, Fat: 12g

Carbs: 6g

Protein: 35g

173. Tumis Labu Siam (Stir-fried Chayote)

Prep Time: 15 mins

Cook Time: 10 mins

Total Time: 25 mins

Servings: 4

Ingredients:

- 2 chayote, peel off, seeded, and julienned
- 1 carrot, julienned
- 2 cloves garlic, chop-up
- 1 mini onion, thinly split
- 1 red chili, split (adjust as needed)
- 1 tbsp oyster sauce
- 1 tbsp soy sauce
- 1/2 tsp sugar
- Salt and pepper as needed
- 2 tbsp vegetable oil

Instructions:

1. In a wok or skillet, heat vegetable oil over medium-high heat
2. Add chop-up onion and chop-up garlic. Stir-fry the onions up to they are transparent and aromatic.
3. Jigged carrot and chayote Must be added. up to they begin to soften, stir-fry for 3 to 4 mins.
4. Add sugar, salt, pepper, oyster sauce, soy sauce, and slices of red chile. Stir-fry the vegetables for a further two to three mins, or up to they are soft but still somewhat crisp.
5. If necessary, adjust the seasoning.
6. Serve the Tumis Labu Siam hot from a serving dish as a side dish

Nutrition (per serving):
Cals: 90, Fat: 5g, Carbs: 10g

Protein: 2g

174. Papeda Kuah Rajungan (Sago Porridge with Crab Soup)

Prep Time: 20 mins

Cook Time: 40 mins

Total Time: 1 hr

Servings: 4

Ingredients:

- 1 cup of sago pearls
- 2 cups of crab meat, cooked and shredded
- 4 cups of seafood or fish stock
- 2 cloves garlic, chop-up
- 1 shallot, chop-up
- 1 lemongrass stalk, smashed
- 2 kaffir lime leaves
- 1 tsp turmeric powder
- 1 tsp salt
- 1/2 tsp white pepper
- 1 cup of coconut milk
- 2 tbsp vegetable oil
- Chop-up cilantro and green onions for garnish

Instructions:

1. Sago pearls Must be cleaned with cold water before being cooked in a pot of boiling water till transparent. Drain. then set apart.
2. Vegetable oil Must be heated over medium heat in a different saucepan. Add shallot and garlic, both chop-up. up to fragrant, sauté.
3. Add fish or seafood stock, chop-up kaffir lime leaves, smashed lemongrass, turmeric powder, salt, and white pepper. To develop the flavors, let it boil for around 20 to 25 mins.
4. Add coconut milk and crab meat. Simmer for a further ten mins.
5. Sago pearls that have been cooked Must be placed in a bowl, then hot crab soup Must be ladled over them.
6. Add chop-up cilantro and green onions as a garnish.
7. Papeda Kuah Rajungan Must be served hot.

Nutrition (per serving):
Cals: 350, Fat: 18g

Carbs: 28g

Protein: 20g

175. Rendang Limpa (Spleen Rendang)

Prep Time: 20 mins

Cook Time: 2 hrs

Total Time: 2 hrs 20 mins

Servings: 4

Ingredients:

- 500g spleen, cleaned and diced
- 2 cups of coconut milk
- 2 lemongrass stalks, bruised
- 3 kaffir lime leaves
- 2 turmeric leaves (non-compulsory), torn
- 2 tbsp oil
- 1 tsp tamarind paste
- Salt and sugar as needed

Instructions:

1. Spleen dice Must be sautéed in hot oil up to just browned.
2. Add the turmeric leaves, kaffir lime leaves, and lemongrass. Stir thoroughly.
3. Add the coconut milk, then boil the Mixture. Let it simmer for roughly an hr, or up to the spleen is soft.
4. Add salt, sugar, and tamarind paste. Once the sauce thickens and the flavors come together, cook it for a further 30 mins.
5. Steamed rice Must be served with the limp rendang.

NUTRITION INFO: (per serving - approximate)
Cals: 300, Protein: 15g

Fat: 20g, Carbs: 15g

Fiber: 2g

176. Kue Serabi Solo (Solo-style Coconut Pancakes)

Prep Time: 15 mins

Cook Time: 20 mins

Total Time: 35 mins

Servings: 8

Ingredients:

- 1 cup of rice flour
- 1/2 cup of all-purpose flour
- 1 cup of coconut milk
- 1/2 cup of water
- 1/4 tsp salt
- 1/4 tsp turmeric powder (for color)
- 2 tbsp granulated sugar
- Finely grated coconut and palm sugar for topping

Instructions:

1. Rice flour, all-purpose flour, coconut milk, water, salt, turmeric powder, and sugar Must be thoroughly combined in a bowl.
2. A ladle of the batter is poured into a preheated nonstick skillet to create a thin pancake.
3. Cook up to the surface begins to set and the edges start to lift. Top with palm sugar and finely grated coconut.

4. The pancake Must be fully cooked after folding it in half and cooking for an additional min.
5. Continue by using the remaining batter.
6. Warm coconut pancakes Must be served.

NUTRITION INFO: (per serving - approximate)
Cals: 150, Protein: 2g

Fat: 6g, Carbs: 22g, Fiber: 1g

177. Sate Udang (Shrimp Satay)

Prep Time: 30 mins

Cook Time: 10 mins

Total Time: 40 mins

Servings: 4

Ingredients:

- 500g Big shrimp, peel off and deveined
- 2 tbsp oil
- 2 cloves garlic, chop-up
- 1 tsp turmeric powder
- 1 tsp coriander powder
- Salt and pepper as needed

Instructions:

1. Combine oil, chop-up garlic, turmeric, coriander, salt, and pepper in a bowl.
2. For 20 to 30 mins, marinate the shrimp in the marinade.
3. The marinated shrimp are threaded onto skewers.
4. Cook and slightly brown the shrimp skewers on the grill or in the pan for two to three mins on every side.
5. Serve rice and peanut sauce beside the shrimp satay.

NUTRITION INFO: (per serving - approximate)
Cals: 180, Protein: 22g

Fat: 8g, Carbs: 3g

Fiber: 0g

178. Soto Lamongan (Lamongan-style Chicken Soup)

Prep Time: 20 mins

Cook Time: 1 hr

Total Time: 1 hr 20 mins

Servings: 6

Ingredients:

- 1 whole chicken, slice into parts
- 2 lemongrass stalks, bruised
- 3 kaffir lime leaves
- 4 cloves garlic, chop-up
- 1 tsp turmeric powder
- 1 tsp coriander powder

- 1 tsp cumin powder
- Salt and pepper as needed
- Rice vermicelli, boiled eggs, and fried shallots for serving

Instructions:
1. Bring enough water to cover the chicken, lemongrass, and kaffir lime leaves to a boil in a pot.
2. Cook the chicken for 30 to 40 mins, then lower the heat to a simmer.
3. Shred the chicken after removing it from the soup.
4. Garlic that has been chop-up, turmeric, coriander, and cumin powder Must all be sautéed up to aromatic in a separate pan.
5. To the broth, add the sautéed spices and the shreds of chicken. Add salt and pepper as needed.
6. Over rice vermicelli, top the soup with fried shallots and boiled eggs as garnish.

NUTRITION INFO: (per serving - approximate)
Cals: 250, Protein: 20g
Fat: 12g, Carbs: 15g, Fiber: 1g

179.Tahu Gimbal (Gimbal Tofu)

Prep Time: 20 mins
Cook Time: 10 mins
Total Time: 30 mins
Servings: 4

Ingredients:
- 300g firm tofu, cubed
- 1 cucumber, julienned
- 2 cups of bean sprouts
- 2 boiled eggs, halved
- 1 cup of white rice, cooked
- 2 tbsp fried shallots
- 1 tbsp tamarind paste
- 2 tbsp sweet soy sauce
- 2 tbsp peanut oil
- Salt as needed

Instructions:
1. Tofu cubes are fried in hot peanut oil up to golden and crispy. Take out, then dry off with paper towels.
2. To make a paste, combine tamarind paste with a little water. Salt and sweet soy sauce are added. To suit your tastes, adjust the flavor.
3. Prepared rice, fried tofu, cucumber, bean sprouts, and boiled eggs Must all be combined in a bowl.
4. Over the ingredients, drizzle the tamarind sauce and top with fried shallots.

5. Serve right away.

Nutrition (per serving):
Cals: ~350 kcal, Protein: ~15g
Carbs: ~40g, Fat: ~15g

180. Sambal Tumpang (East Javanese Chili Sauce)

Prep Time: 15 mins
Cook Time: 15 mins
Total Time: 30 mins
Servings: About 1 cup of

Ingredients:
- 10 red chilies, seeded and chop-up
- 5 shallots, chop-up
- 3 cloves garlic, chop-up
- 1 tomato, chop-up
- 1 tsp shrimp paste (terasi), toasted
- 1 tsp palm sugar or brown sugar
- Salt as needed
- 1 tbsp vegetable oil

Instructions:
1. Shallots, garlic, and chiles are sautéed in hot oil up to aromatic.
2. Cook the tomato up to it softens before adding the tomato and shrimp paste.
3. Take out the Mixture from the heat and let it to cool slightly.
4. Put the Mixture in a mortar and pestle together with the salt and palm sugar, and grind to a paste.
5. Use as a condiment or dipping sauce.

Nutrition (per tbsp):
Cals: ~20 kcal, Protein: ~0.5g
Carbs: ~3g, Fat: ~1g

181. Bubur Ketan Putih (White Glutinous Rice Porridge)

Prep Time: 2 hrs (for soaking)
Cook Time: 1 hr
Total Time: 3 hrs
Servings: 6

Ingredients:
- 1 cup of white glutinous rice, soaked for 2 hrs
- 4 cups of coconut milk
- 1 pandan leaf, knotted
- 1/2 cup of sugar
- 1/2 tsp salt
- Toppings: coconut cream, split mango, toasted sesame seeds

Instructions:

1. Rinse the sticky rice thoroughly after draining.
2. Glutinous rice, coconut milk, pandan leaf, sugar, and salt Must all be combined in a pot.
3. Stirring occasionally, cook the rice over low heat up to it is cooked and the porridge has thickened.
4. Take the pandan leaf off.
5. Serve the porridge in bowls with split mango, toasted sesame seeds, and a dollop of coconut cream on top.

Nutrition (per serving):
Cals: ~350 kcal, Protein: ~3g
Carbs: ~45g, Fat: ~18g

182. Papeda Kuah Udang (Sago Porridge with Shrimp Soup)

Prep Time: 2 hrs (for soaking)
Cook Time: 30 mins
Total Time: 2 hrs 30 mins
Servings: 4

Ingredients:

- 1 cup of sago pearls, soaked for 2 hrs
- 500g shrimp, peel off and deveined
- 4 cups of water
- 2 lemongrass stalks, bruised
- 4 kaffir lime leaves
- 1 tsp turmeric powder
- Salt as needed
- Lime wedges for serving

Instructions:

1. Bring the water to a boil in a pot. Add the turmeric powder, lemongrass, kaffir lime leaves, and shrimp. around ten mins, simmer.
2. While constantly swirling to avoid sticking, add the soaked sago pearls to the pot.
3. Cook the sago pearls up to they become translucent and the porridge thickens.
4. As needed, add salt to the dish.
5. Serve the heated porridge with lime wedges as a garnish.

Nutrition (per serving):
Cals: ~220 kcal, Protein: ~15g
Carbs: ~25g, Fat: ~6g

183. Kue Lumpur Bandung (Bandung-style Mud Cake)

Prep Time: 20 mins
Cook Time: 40 mins
Total Time: 1 hr
Servings: 8

Ingredients:

- 200 grams glutinous rice flour
- 50 grams all-purpose flour
- 200 grams palm sugar, finely grated
- 400 ml coconut milk
- 1/2 tsp salt
- 2 pandan leaves, knotted
- Finely grated cheese for topping

Instructions:

1. Combine all-purpose flour and glutinous rice flour in a bowl.
2. Coconut milk, palm sugar, salt, and pandan leaves are heated in a saucepan over medium heat up to the palm sugar dissolves. Don't let it to boil.
3. Add the flour Mixture to the pot gradually while constantly stirring to prevent lumps. Cook the Mixture up to it thickens.
4. Set the oven's temperature to 180 C (350 F).
5. Place about 3/4 of the Mixture into every of the mini heatproof cups of or cup ofcake molds.
6. The molds Must be placed on a baking sheet and baked for 20 to 25 mins in a preheated oven, or up to the tops are set and a toothpick inserted comes out clean.
7. Take them out of the oven, then let them cool.
8. After it has cooled, sprinkle finely grated cheese on top and serve.

Nutrition (per serving):
Cals: 250 kcal, Carbs: 38 g
Protein: 3 g, Fat: 10 g, Fiber: 1 g

184. Sate Kuda (Horse Satay)

Prep Time: 30 mins
Cook Time: 15 mins
Total Time: 45 mins
Servings: 4

Ingredients:

- 500 grams horse meat, slice into mini cubes
- 1 tbsp vegetable oil
- 2 shallots, lightly chop-up
- 2 cloves garlic, chop-up
- 1 tsp turmeric powder
- 1 tsp coriander powder
- 1/2 tsp cumin powder
- 1 tsp brown sugar
- Salt and pepper as needed
- Bamboo skewers, soaked in water

Instructions:

1. To make the marinade, combine the vegetable oil, shallots, garlic, turmeric, coriander, and

cumin powders, along with brown sugar, salt, and pepper in a bowl.

2. Combine thoroughly before adding the cubes of horse meat to the marinade. Give it at least one hr to marinate.

3. Onto the moistened bamboo skewers, thread the marinated horse meat.

4. For about 10-15 mins, flip the skewers on a grill pan or barbeque over medium-high heat up to the meat is thoroughly cooked and gently browned.

5. Serve rice and peanut sauce beside the horse satay.

Nutrition (per serving):
Cals: 250 kcal, Carbs: 5 g

Protein: 25 g, Fat: 15 g, Fiber: 1 g

185. Soto Bandung (Bandung-style Chicken Soup)

Prep Time: 20 mins

Cook Time: 1 hr

Total Time: 1 hr 20 mins

Servings: 6

Ingredients:

- 1 whole chicken (about 1.5 kg), slice into pieces
- 2 lemongrass stalks, bruised
- 3 kaffir lime leaves
- 2 bay leaves
- 4 cloves garlic, chop-up
- 2 shallots, chop-up
- 1 tsp ground turmeric
- 1 tsp ground coriander
- Salt and pepper as needed
- 150 grams glass noodles, soaked in hot water
- 100 grams bean sprouts
- Fried shallots for garnish
- Hard-boiled eggs, halved
- Lime wedges
- Chop-up cilantro

Instructions:

1. Chicken chunks, lemongrass, kaffir lime leaves, bay leaves, garlic, shallots, ground turmeric, ground coriander, salt, and pepper Must all be placed in a big pot.

2. The chicken Must be covered with water. Cook for 45–60 mins, or up to the chicken is cooked, after bringing to a boil and then lowering the heat to a simmer.

3. Shred the chicken after removing the pieces from the broth.

4. To serve, divide the glass noodles, bean sprouts, and chicken into individual bowls.

5. Over the contents in every bowl, ladle the hot broth.

6. Add fried shallots, boiled eggs, lime wedges, and chop-up cilantro as garnishes.

Nutrition (per serving):
Cals: 300 kcal, Carbs: 25 g

Protein: 25 g, Fat: 10 g, Fiber: 2 g

186. Nasi Krawu (East Javanese Rice Dish)

Prep Time: 30 mins

Cook Time: 30 mins

Total Time: 1 hr

Servings: 4

Ingredients:

- 2 cups of cooked white rice
- 200 grams beef, thinly split and marinated with sweet soy sauce
- 200 grams shredded coconut, toasted
- 4 boiled eggs, halved
- Sambal (chili sauce)
- 2 tbsp vegetable oil
- 2 shallots, thinly split
- 2 cloves garlic, chop-up
- 1 lemongrass stalk, bruised
- 2 bay leaves
- Salt and sugar as needed
- Split cucumber and tomato for garnish

Instructions:

1. In a pan, heat the vegetable oil on medium. The bay leaves, lemongrass, shallots, and garlic Must be sautéed up to aromatic.

2. Cook the beef, stirring occasionally, up to browned and well cooked.

3. As needed, add salt and sugar to the dish.

4. Put some cooked rice on a platter to be served.

5. Around the rice, place the boiled eggs, split cucumber, tomato, and cooked beef.

6. Sambal Must be served on the side.

Nutrition (per serving):
Cals: 450 kcal, Carbs: 40 g

Protein: 18 g, Fat: 25 g, Fiber: 3 g

187.Sambal Tempoyak (Fermented Durian Chili Sauce)

Prep Time: 15 mins

Cook Time: 30 mins

Total Time: 45 mins

Servings: 6

Ingredients:

- 2 cups of durian flesh, fermented and mashed
- 10 red chili peppers, deseeded and split
- 5 shallots, chop-up
- 4 cloves garlic, chop-up
- 1 tsp shrimp paste
- 2 tbsp tamarind pulp
- 1 tsp sugar
- Salt as needed
- Oil for sautéing

Instructions:

1. Shallots and garlic Must be sautéed in hot oil up to aromatic.
2. Add shrimp paste and thinly split chile peppers. Peppers Must be sautéed up to they are tender.
3. Add mashed tamarind pulp and durian flesh. Stir thoroughly, then simmer for a short while.
4. Depending on your taste, add salt and sugar to the dish.
5. Before serving, take out the sambal tempoyak from the fire and let it to cool.

Nutrition (per serving):
Cals: 120, Protein: 2g

Fat: 6g, Carbs: 15g

Fiber: 3g

188. Tumis Jamur Tiram (Stir-fried Oyster Mushrooms)

Prep Time: 10 mins

Cook Time: 15 mins

Total Time: 25 mins

Servings: 4

Ingredients:

- 500g oyster mushrooms, cleaned and split
- 1 onion, thinly split
- 2 cloves garlic, chop-up
- 1 red bell pepper, julienned
- 1 green bell pepper, julienned
- 2 tbsp soy sauce
- 1 tbsp oyster sauce
- 1 tsp sugar
- Salt and pepper as needed
- Oil for cooking

Instructions:

1. Garlic and onion are sautéed in hot oil up to aromatic.
2. Stir-fry the oyster mushrooms after adding them up to they begin to soften.
3. For a few mins longer, stir-fry the red and green bell peppers.

4. Add sugar, salt, pepper, oyster sauce, and soy sauce. To evenly cover the mushrooms and vegetables, stir thoroughly.
5. Cook for a few more mins, or up to the Mixture is well heated.
6. Steamed rice Must be served with the stir-fried oyster mushrooms.

Nutrition (per serving):
Cals: 80, Protein: 5g, Fat: 2g

Carbs: 12g, Fiber: 3g

189. Papeda Kuah Cumi (Sago Porridge with Squid Soup)

Prep Time: 15 mins

Cook Time: 45 mins

Total Time: 1 hr

Servings: 4

Ingredients:

- 200g squid, cleaned and slice into rings
- 1 cup of sago pearls
- 4 cups of water
- 2 cloves garlic, chop-up
- 1 shallot, chop-up
- 2 tbsp cooking oil
- Salt as needed
- Pepper as needed
- Lime wedges for serving

Instructions:

1. Sago pearls Must be drained after a cold water rinse.
2. Bring 4 cups of water to a boil in a kettle. Sago pearls Must be added and cooked for 15-20 mins, or up to they are transparent and tender. To avoid sticking, stir every so while. Drain, then set apart.
3. Cooking oil Must be warmed up in a separate saucepan over medium heat. Sauté the shallot and chop-up garlic up to fragrant.
4. Squid rings Must be added and cooked for two to three mins, or up to opaque.
5. 4 cups of water Must be added before simmering the Mixture. Let it to simmer for 20 to 25 mins.
6. Add salt and pepper as needed when preparing the soup.
7. Sago pearls that have been cooked Must be placed in a bowl, then the squid soup Must be ladled over them. Lime wedges Must be served alongside.

Nutrition (per serving):
Cals: 220 kcal, Protein: 10g

Fat: 8g, Carbs: 28g, Fiber: 1g

190. Rendang Babat (Tripe Rendang)

Prep Time: 20 mins

Cook Time: 2 hrs

Total Time: 2 hrs 20 mins

Servings: 6

Ingredients:

- 500g tripe, cleaned and slice into bite-sized pieces
- 2 cups of coconut milk
- 2 stalks lemongrass, bruised
- 3 kaffir lime leaves
- 2 turmeric leaves (non-compulsory), torn into pieces
- Salt as needed
- Banana leaves for wrapping (if available)
- Spice Paste:
- 5 shallots
- 3 cloves garlic
- 2 red chilies (adjust for spice level)
- 1 thumb-sized ginger
- 1 thumb-sized galangal
- 1 tsp turmeric powder
- 1 tsp coriander powder
- 1 tsp cumin powder

Instructions:

1. The spice paste ingredients Must be processed in a mixer up to smooth.
2. Heat a little oil in a pot, then sauté the spice paste up to it is aromatic.
3. When the tripe pieces are thoroughly coated with the spice paste, add them and sauté for a few mins.
4. Add the lemongrass, kaffir lime leaves, and turmeric leaves after adding the coconut milk. To blend, stir.
5. For about 1.5 to 2 hrs, or up to the tripe is soft and the sauce thickens, simmer the dish with the lid on over low heat.
6. To keep the rendang from burning and sticking, stir it occasionally. For more flavor, wrap the rendang in banana leaves while it's cooking if you're using them.
7. Add salt as needed once the rendang is soft and the sauce has thickened.
8. Serve steamed rice alongside the Rendang Babat.

Nutrition (per serving):

Cals: 320 kcal, Protein: 15g

Fat: 26g, Carbs: 8g

Fiber: 2g

191. Kue Cucur Solo (Solo-style Fried Pancake with Palm Sugar)

Prep Time: 15 mins

Cook Time: 20 mins

Total Time: 35 mins

Servings: 8

Ingredients:

- 1 cup of rice flour
- 1/4 cup of all-purpose flour
- 1/2 tsp baking powder
- 1/2 tsp turmeric powder
- 1 cup of coconut milk
- 1/4 cup of water
- 1/4 tsp salt
- Oil for frying
- Palm sugar (gula jawa) for filling
- Finely grated coconut for garnish

Instructions:

1. Rice flour, all-purpose flour, baking powder, and turmeric powder Must all be combined in a combining basin.
2. To create a smooth batter, gradually add the coconut milk and water while stirring. Combine thoroughly after adding salt. Ten mins Must be given for the batter to rest.
3. In a non-stick pan, warm a little oil over medium heat.
4. To make a round pancake, spoon some batter onto the pan. Cook up to the bottom turns golden brown and the edges begin to rise.
5. The pancake Must be centered with a little piece of palm sugar, then it Must be folded over to enclose the sugar. Using pressure, close the edges.
6. The pancake Must be cooked up to golden and crispy on both sides.
7. The pancake Must be taken out of the pan and dried on paper towels.
8. Warm Kue Cucur Solo Must be served with finely grated coconut on top as a garnish.

Nutrition (per serving):

Cals: 180 kcal, Protein: 2g

Fat: 6g, Carbs: 30g

Fiber: 1g

192. Sate Kerbau Batak (Batak-style Buffalo Satay)

Prep Time: 30 mins (+ marinating time)

Cook Time: 15 mins

Total Time: 45 mins (+ marinating time)

Servings: 4

Ingredients:

- 500g buffalo meat, slice into mini cubes
- 1 onion, finely grated
- 3 cloves garlic, chop-up
- 1 tsp ground turmeric
- 1 tsp ground coriander
- 1 tsp ground cumin
- 1 tsp chili powder (adjust for spice level)
- Salt and pepper as needed
- Bamboo skewers, soaked in water

Instructions:

1. To make a marinade, combine the chop-up garlic, chili powder, salt, pepper, turmeric, ground coriander, and ground cumin in a bowl.
2. Make sure the buffalo meat cubes are thoroughly covered before adding them to the marinade. For at least two hrs and ideally overnight, cover and chill the dish.
3. The soaking bamboo skewers are then threaded with the marinated meat.
4. A grill or grill pan Must be preheated to high heat.
5. The buffalo skewers Must be cooked and slightly browned after around 10-15 mins of grilling, rotating the skewers occasionally.
6. Serve the Sate Kerbau Batak hot with steaming rice and your preferred dipping sauce.

Nutrition (per serving):
Cals: 220 kcal, Protein: 30g

Fat: 8g, Carbs: 5g

Fiber: 1g

193. Papeda Kuah Tenggiri (Sago Porridge with Spanish Mackerel Soup)

Prep Time: 20 mins

Cook Time: 1 hr

Total Time: 1 hr 20 mins

Servings: 4

Ingredients:

- 200g sago pearls
- 300g Spanish mackerel fillets, slice into chunks
- 1 liter water
- 2 stalks lemongrass, bruised
- 3 kaffir lime leaves
- 2 slices galangal
- Salt as needed

Instructions:

1. Sago pearls Must be drained after a cold water rinse.
2. Bring the water to a boil in a pot. Sago pearls Must be added and cooked while stirring constantly up to transparent. It ought to take 20 to 25 mins. Drain, then set apart.
3. Bring water to a boil in another pot. Add the lemongrass, kaffir lime leaves, galangal, and slices of Spanish mackerel. Making the fish broth requires around 30 mins of simmering. Take out and throw away the aromatics.
4. The fish broth will continue to simmer for an additional 10 to 15 mins after you add the cooked sago pearls.
5. Salt the oatmeal to your preferred taste.
6. If preferred, add additional lime wedges and chop-up cilantro to the Papeda Kuah Tenggiri while serving.

Nutrition (per serving):
Cals: 250 kcal, Protein: 15g

Fat: 8g, Carbs: 30g

Fiber: 2g

194. Rendang Lidah (Tongue Rendang)

Prep Time: 30 mins

Cook Time: 3 hrs

Total Time: 3 hrs 30 mins

Servings: 6

Ingredients:

- 1 beef tongue, cleaned and split
- 400ml coconut milk
- 2 lemongrass stalks, bruised
- 4 kaffir lime leaves
- 2 turmeric leaves (non-compulsory)
- 2 tamarind slices
- Salt and sugar as needed
- Banana leaves for wrapping (non-compulsory)

Instructions:

1. Bring water to a boil in a pot. Add the beef tongue slices and blanch for 5 mins approximately. Take out and wash with ice-cold water. This aids in the removal of pollutants and extra fat.
2. The blanched beef tongue, coconut milk, lemongrass, kaffir lime leaves, turmeric leaves, and tamarind slices Must all be combined in a different saucepan.
3. Stirring occasionally, cook the Mixture over low heat up to the sauce has thickened and the beef tongue is soft. It ought to take two to three hrs.

4. You can add salt and sugar to the rendang to suit your taste.
5. Wrap the rendang in banana leaves if you're using them, then steam it for an additional 10 to 15 mins to let the flavors meld.
6. Serve steamed rice alongside the Rendang Lidah.

Nutrition (per serving):
Cals: 380 kcal, Protein: 25g

Fat: 30g, Carbs: 8g, Fiber: 2g

195. Sambal Roa (Smoked Fish Chili Sauce)

Prep Time: 15 mins

Cook Time: 15 mins

Total Time: 30 mins

Servings: 8

Ingredients:
- 150g smoked fish (roa), flaked
- 10 red chili peppers, deseeded and chop-up
- 5 shallots, chop-up
- 4 cloves garlic, chop-up
- 1 tomato, chop-up
- 1 tsp shrimp paste (terasi), toasted
- Salt and sugar as needed
- Juice of 1 lime

Instructions:
1. Chop-up chili peppers, shallots, garlic, tomatoes, and toasted shrimp paste Must be combined to make a paste in a mortar and pestle.
2. The paste Must be sautéed in a mini amount of hot oil up to aromatic.
3. In the pan, combine the paste thoroughly with the flaked smoked salmon.
4. You can adjust the amount of salt, sugar, and lime juice in the sambal to suit your taste.
5. Cook for a further 5-7 mins, stirring periodically, to thoroughly blend the flavors.
6. Serve rice or other foods with the Sambal Roa as a hot condiment.

Nutrition (per serving):
Cals: 70 kcal, Protein: 6g

Fat: 3g, Carbs: 6g, Fiber: 1g

196. Tumis Kacang Panjang (Stir-fried Yardlong Beans)

Prep Time: 10 mins

Cook Time: 15 mins

Total Time: 25 mins

Servings: 4

Ingredients:
- 300g yardlong beans (kacang panjang), slice into 3-inch pieces
- 2 cloves garlic, chop-up
- 2 shallots, split
- 2 red chili peppers, split
- 1 tsp shrimp paste (terasi)
- 1 tbsp soy sauce
- 1 tsp oyster sauce
- Salt and sugar as needed

Instructions:
1. Oil in a pan is heated to medium heat. Include the chop-up garlic, shallots, and red chili peppers in slices. up to fragrant, sauté.
2. Sauté for another min after adding the shrimp paste.
3. The yardlong beans Must be tender but still have a tiny crunch, so add them to the pan and stir-fry for roughly 5-7 mins.
4. Depending on your taste, you can add soy sauce, oyster sauce, salt, and sugar to the beans' seasoning.
5. Once the flavors are well-balanced and the beans are thoroughly cooked, stir-fry for an additional 2-3 mins.
6. With steamed rice, serve the Tumis Kacang Panjang as a delectable side dish.

Nutrition (per serving):
Cals: 60 kcal, Protein: 2g

Fat: 2g, Carbs: 10g, Fiber: 3g

197. Papeda Kuah Rajungan (Sago Porridge with Crab Soup)

Prep Time: 20 mins

Cook Time: 1 hr

Total Time: 1 hr 20 mins

Servings: 4

Ingredients:
- 200g sago pearls
- 2 crabs, cleaned and slice into pieces
- 1 lemongrass stalk, bruised
- 2 kaffir lime leaves
- 4 cloves garlic, chop-up
- 2 shallots, chop-up
- 1 tsp turmeric powder
- 1 tsp ginger paste
- 1 tsp salt
- 1/2 tsp white pepper
- 1 liter water
- 2 tbsp cooking oi
- Fresh cilantro leaves for garnish

Instructions:

1. Bring water to a boil in a pot. Sago pearls are added, cooked till transparent while being stirred infrequently. Drain, then set apart.
2. Cooking oil Must be heated on medium heat in a separate saucepan. Shallots and chop-up garlic are cooked up to aromatic.
3. Salt, white pepper, ginger paste, and turmeric powder Must be added. Stir thoroughly.
4. When the crab pieces turn red, add them to the stew and boil for a few mins.
5. Lemongrass stalk and kaffir lime leaves Must be added, along with 1 liter of water. 30 to 40 mins after bringing to a simmer.
6. Take out the lemongrass and kaffir lime leaves once the crab has been cooked and the flavors have come together.
7. To serve, spoon some fried sago pearls into a bowl and top with the crab soup.
8. Before serving, garnish with fresh cilantro leaves.

198. Rendang Paru (Lung Rendang)

Prep Time: 15 mins

Cook Time: 2 hrs

Total Time: 2 hrs 15 mins

Servings: 6

Ingredients:

- 500g beef lung (paru), cleaned and split
- 2 cups of coconut milk
- 2 lemongrass stalks, bruised
- 2 kaffir lime leaves
- 2 bay leaves
- 3 tbsp rendang spice paste (can be store-bought or homemade)
- 1 tsp tamarind paste
- 1 tsp salt
- 1 tsp sugar
- 2 tbsp cooking oil

Instructions:

1. In a pan, heat the cooking oil on medium. The rendang spice paste Must be cooked up to aromatic.
2. Split beef lung Must be added to the pan and stir-fried for a few mins up to beginning to brown.
3. Add the bay leaves, lemongrass, and kaffir lime leaves after pouring in the coconut milk. Stir thoroughly.
4. After bringing the Mixture to a simmer, lower the heat. Let it to simmer uncovered for about 1-2 hrs, stirring regularly, or up to the coconut milk has thickened and the lung is soft.

5. Add salt, sugar, and tamarind paste. To let the flavors to mingle, simmer for a further 10-15 mins.
6. Take out from heat once the rendang has reveryed the proper consistency and the lung is tender.
7. With steamed rice or other typical Indonesian side dishes, serve the rendang paru.

199.Soto Makassar (Makassar-style Beef Soup)

Prep Time: 20 mins

Cook Time: 2 hrs

Total Time: 2 hrs 20 mins

Servings: 4

Ingredients:

- 500g beef shank, slice into chunks
- 2 liters water
- 2 lemongrass stalks, bruised
- 3 kaffir lime leaves
- 2 bay leaves
- 2 cloves
- 2 cardamom pods
- 2 cinnamon sticks
- Salt and pepper as needed
- 3 potatoes, peel off and slice into chunks
- 200g rice vermicelli, cooked according to box/pkg instructions
- 4 boiled eggs, halved
- Fried shallots for garnish
- Chop-up fresh cilantro for garnish
- Lime wedges for serving

Instructions:

1. Beef, water, lemongrass, kaffir lime leaves, bay leaves, cloves, cardamom pods, cinnamon sticks, salt, and pepper Must all be combined in a big pot. Bring to a boil, lower the heat to a simmer, and cook the Mixture for 1.5 to 2 hrs, or up to the meat is cooked.
2. Using forks, take out the beef from the soup and shred it. Place aside.
3. Add the potatoes to the same saucepan and boil them up to they are fork-tender.
4. Put some cooked rice vermicelli in a bowl to serve. Add cooked potatoes, boiling egg halves, and beef that has been chop-up.
5. Pour the boiling beef broth over the bowl's components.
6. Add chop-up cilantro and fried shallots as a garnish.
7. Lime wedges and sambal terasi hijau (green shrimp paste chili sauce) Must be served alongside the dish.

NUTRITION INFO:

Cals: ~400 per serving

Protein: ~20g, Carbs: ~40g

Fat: ~15g

200.Sambal Terasi Hijau (Green Shrimp Paste Chili Sauce)

Prep Time: 15 mins
Cook Time: 5 mins
Total Time: 20 mins
Servings: Makes about 1 cup of

Ingredients:

- 10 green bird's eye chilies, stems take outd
- 3 cloves garlic
- 2 tsp shrimp paste (terasi), toasted
- 1 tsp sugar
- Juice of 1 lime
- Salt as needed

Instructions:

1. Grind the green chilies, garlic, and toasted shrimp paste into a smooth Mixture in a mortar and pestle.
2. Include salt, lime juice, and sugar. Combine thoroughly up to sugar melts.
3. The seasoning Must be tasted and adjusted as necessary by adding extra salt, sugar, or lime juice.
4. Put the sambal terasi in a bowl for serving.

NUTRITION INFO:

Cals: ~15 per tbsp

Protein: ~0.5g, Carbs: ~3g

Fat: ~0.5g

Made in the USA
Columbia, SC
11 February 2025

53697597R00043